Jamaica
The fairest isle

A visitor's guide

Philip Sherlock and Barbara Preston

CARIBBEAN

First published 1992

Published by MACMILLAN EDUCATION LTD
London and Basingstoke
*Associated companies and representatives in Accra,
Auckland, Delhi, Dublin, Gaborone, Hamburg, Harare,
Hong Kong, Kuala Lumpur, Lagos, Manzini, Melbourne,
Mexico City, Nairobi, New York, Singapore, Tokyo*

ISBN 0 – 333 – 56438 – 3

Printed in Hong Kong

A catalogue record for this book is available from
the British Library.

| Contents |

| Acknowledgements |

The authors wish to acknowledge with sincere thanks the valuable assistance given by The Jamaica Tourist Board, and especially by:
Mr Noel Mignott, Deputy Director of Tourism, Marketing and Administration, New York
Miss Vinton Spencer, Chief Editor
Mrs Madge Allen, Area Manager, Mandeville and the South Coast
Staff of the Product Department in Negril, Montego Bay, Ocho Rios, Port Antonio and Kingston
Mrs Leeta Hearne, Editor, The Jamaica Journal
The Negril Chamber of Commerce

The authors are grateful to the following for assistance given with photographs:
Sistren Theatre Collective
Andreas Oberli
Jackie Scott
Herbie Gordon
Martin Mordecai
Caroline Lee
Theo Smit
Oliver Benn (front cover)
G.W. Lennox (back cover)

The authors and publishers are grateful to George Allen and Unwin (Publishers) Ltd for permission to reproduce two extracts from *Waters of the West* by Kenneth Pringle; to Dr Omar Davis and Dr Michael Witter for quotations from *The Development of the Jamaican Economy since Independence* and to the Institute of Jamaica for quotations from *From Our Yard*.

| 1 |
Keeping company with Jamaica

Jamaicans speak two languages, Jamaica Talk and English. Jamaica Talk is for family and friends and for communicating with other Jamaicans. It is also for abuse, being rich in vivid imagery and devastating epithets.

In Jamaica Talk 'to keep company with someone' means much more than to accompany him or her. It means to be in tune with another person. It is warm, intimate. It tells of a journey to a destination and to the heart.

This book is for those who wish to keep company with Jamaica; who wish to combine sight-seeing with insight; who wish to make two journeys, one through a beautiful country and the other into the Jamaican way of life. It shows how to transform a visit into a discovery.

Discovery begins with arrival. A travel writer has described the process. Having passed through immigration and customs at the Norman Manley airport, which is on a narrow finger of land that almost encircles Kingston Harbour, he was on his way into the city by taxi:

> Driving along a road choked with honking traffic, I suddenly saw a strange man, all arms and legs and very thin and wearing one of those incongruous caps, walking blithely along as if on a tight rope.
>
> 'What on earth is he doing there?' I asked the driver.
>
> 'Man,' he replied, 'he just walking along the white line. Why not?'
>
> I knew I was back in Jamaica, the country of the individual who won't be a carbon copy of anyone. In Jamaica the barman who serves you talks to you on a plane of total and unstudied equality. Some visitors don't like this, and my advice to them is that they should go somewhere else. Which would be a pity since they would miss one of the loveliest island countries in the world.

Jamaicans are characterised by individualism, and a tender yet fiercely possessive love of their country. The odds are that within an hour of your arrival a Jamaican, the taxi-driver maybe or the bell captain at the hotel, will ask 'How you like Jamaica?' The wise course is not to waste time explaining that you have just arrived but to declare, 'I have fallen in love with your country already.' This may well be true, for Jamaica takes possession of its visitors very quickly.

The first step in keeping company with Jamaica is to sweep away the clutter of clichés and slogans produced by the image-makers. Jamaicans resent stereotypes of themselves and their fellow West Indians as calypso singers and bongo drummers wearing fixed smiles and broad-rimmed hats. Struggling hard against poverty, they dislike talk about a 'tropical paradise'. Posters depicting palm trees, wide beaches and narrow bikinis lead them to insist, 'We're more than a beach, we're a country.' How much more sincere are the words the Elizabethan sailor John Sparke wrote more than three centuries ago, that Jamaica is 'a country marvelously sweet'.

The island challenges the visitor to get away from the beaten track and to explore its hidden valleys; to discover spectacular retreats like Cinchona and the coffee country round about Mavis Bank and Arntully; to go by canoe through the waterways of Swamp; to visit the Spas at Bath, Milk River and Sans Souci, all more efficacious than the waters of Baden-Baden; to explore caves and to scuba-dive along the offshore reefs.

The challenge is to explore oneself as well, to open up the mind and senses to a new physical and cultural environment. Thoreau would approve. 'Explore your own higher altitudes . . . Nay, be a Columbus to whole new continents and worlds within you, opening new channels not of trade but of thought.'

How is it that, though Jamaica is an island to which many tourists come, it is not a tourist island?

In part, it is because of the nature of the people and in part because of the mountains. The island is the top of a drowned mountain range. Between it and Cuba lies the Bartlett Trough, which is more than 20 000 feet deep in places. If the sea were drained away, Blue Mountain Peak, 7400 feet above sea-level, would almost rival Mount Everest.

Friendship *opposite* [JAMAICA TOURIST BOARD]

The extraordinary thing is that the land sweeps upward so swiftly. The island is only a hundred and forty-six miles long and fifty-three miles across at the widest part. From Kingston to Port Antonio, as the crow flies, is only twenty miles. Yet that narrow space is packed tight with the highest peaks in the islands of the Commonwealth Caribbean: with Catherine's Peak, Stoddard's Peak, Half a Bottle, Corn Puss Gap and Blue Mountain Peak.

To get an unforgettable picture of the island, fly from Montego Bay to Kingston; or from Ocho Rios or Port Antonio. Try for a clear morning, before the clouds start gathering. From the plane you will

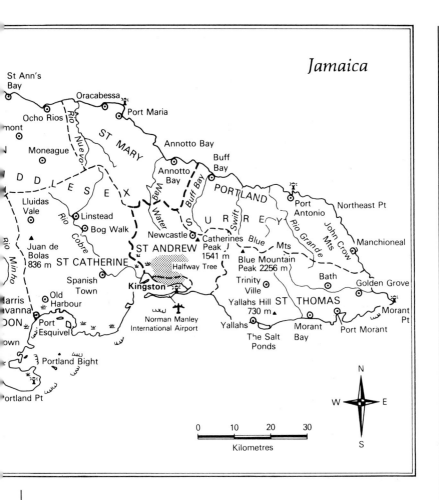

Jamaica

see how the central range and the ridges and spurs that branch out laterally split Jamaica into an archipelago, with an encircled saucer of fertile land here, a confusion of hills there, and scattered pasture-lands. Seeing the many divisions, it is easy to understand how it is that, though Jamaicans identify with Jamaica, each identifies also with his own parish (a St James man, a St Elizabeth woman, a Portlander and so on) and with a particular district or village where he still has 'family' or owns a share of the 'family land'.

The mountains mould the island's many faces. They account for the variations in elevation, climate, rainfall and soil. The misty

5

valleys of the Rio Grande in Portland are lush wet tropics and, to the south, on the other side of the mountain range, is the gaunt cactus landscape of the Hellshire Hills just to the west of Kingston.

An hour's driving takes the visitor from wet tropics to dry; from hot lowlands to cool hill country; from the wind-cooled north coast to cold green pastures and 'the stunted pine trees of mountain Jamaica with strawberries and conifers'; from housing developments and estates to cattle country, smallholdings and mountain settlements.

Through these close-set contrasts Jamaica captures all the senses: sight, hearing, taste, smell and touch. Memory being the most lasting and precious part of any vacation, some sounds and scents bring back special occasions: evenings in a garden above Ocho Rios with the star-jasmine in flower; a road near Mandeville fragrant with orange blossoms; the pungent sweet-sour smell of a newly-harvested field of sugar-cane near Rose Hall; the scent of coffee being parched in the outside kitchen of a country cottage; the spicy tang of pimento; the smell of pork and chicken barbecued over pimento logs; fish being fried at wayside stalls; the turpentine-smell of ripe mangoes; the clamour of a country market; the shrill music of cicadas at sundown time; a mocking bird pouring out its heart from the topmost branch of a poinciana tree; and in city and country village the sound of reggae, of Bob Marley's 'By the rivers of Babylon' and 'No Woman, nuh cry' and of his other songs which have touched the heart of the world.

There are other sounds and smells to be listed. The unmistakable smell of ganja or marijuana; the crowing of roosters that greet the dawn three hours or so before it is due; dogs that bark through the long hours of the night and donkeys that bray on the hour. These all have their place in Jamaica.

Opening our senses to the physical environment of land, sea and air, we find that the country has a rhythm of its own and that the landscape is not a splendid backdrop or stage setting, but an essential part of the Jamaican way of life. People and land are a harmony. Skin tones, gesture, language, music and dance repeat and recreate the rhythm to which life moves, relaxed yet at times intense, with its own pace, its own unique modes of expression. The Caribbean world breaks in upon us, a world of hubbub and laughter, of people

In the Blue Mountains *opposite* [ANDREAS OBERLI]

6

who speak with the whole body, eyes and face, arms, shoulders, torso and hips, filling each word with drama.

But Jamaica is more than a glorious landscape. Keeping company with Jamaica involves finding out something about the Jamaican experience; learning how Jamaicans are grappling with unemployment; how they are trying to strengthen their economy and improve the standard of living of the people; how they are struggling to provide their children with a better future.

This book is written in the hope that the visitor will not allow the beauty of the land to blind him to something more significant, the emergence of a dynamic society of free people.

In forty years – a short time in the life of a nation – Jamaicans have created a national identity, used their political power with sophistication and good judgement, shown the ability to manage their affairs and are creating forms of artistic and cultural expression which have their roots in the indigenous and not in the imported. More than anything else Jamaicans ask their visitors to see how, out of a past of fire, suffering and neglect, their spirit has survived and is now expressing itself through the dynamism of a creative society.

Those visitors who understand this find it easy to relate to Jamaicans. They understand why Jamaicans object to being called 'natives'. The word recalls a colonial society in which there were the 'rulers', superiors from overseas, and the inferior 'natives'. They understand also that, whereas Americans express friendliness and acceptance of others by using first names at their first meeting, Jamaicans are more formal. In their history the use of the first name was often a mark of inferior status. One begins with 'Mr' or 'Miss' or 'Lady' or 'Sir' as a mark of respect and status. Once that has been established, the use of first names follows. By then it is a sign of acceptance and friendship.

For Jamaicans respond quickly to friendship. Many of them have relatives overseas, in the United States, Canada and England. They enjoy talking about other lands and people as well as about their own country. 'Man,' they will tell you, 'travel is the best education.' And perhaps one will quote the Jamaican proverb 'if crab nuh walk, him don't grow claw', which means, 'if a crab doesn't move around he won't grow claws'.

| 2 |
The island, its plants and animals

The first dwellers in Jamaica, the Arawak Indians, gave Jamaica its name, Xaymaca, which probably meant 'land of springs'. When Columbus discovered the island he named it St Jago (Santiago). Fortunately the old name survived and gradually displaced St Jago.

Jamaica is the third largest of the fifty-one inhabited islands in the Caribbean archipelago. Cuba is largest, with 44 000 square miles, one-half the total land area. Haiti and the Dominican Republic share the second largest island, Hispaniola, which is 30 000 square miles in area. Jamaica has an area of 4400 square miles, and is a third larger than Puerto Rico, which comes fourth with 3400 square miles. The other forty-seven islands share the remaining 7000 square miles. Nowhere else in the Americas is there such imbalance in size between countries, and no other New World countries are affected so harshly by economies of scale.

The four large islands, the Greater Antilles, make up the western half of the archipelago. Jamaica lies just inside the rim, ninety miles south of eastern Cuba. It has considerable strategic value, for it is centrally placed. It is equidistant – five hundred miles – from Miami, San Juan and Colon, and it commands some of the chief sea-routes of the Caribbean. Its strategic value was even greater in the days of sailing ships, so much so that after the English took it from Spain in 1655 a Spanish diplomat described it as 'a dagger pointed at the soft underbelly of Spanish America'.

It is part of Jamaica's charm that it is not in the 'big island league'; large islands, like continents, are not collectible. They cannot be taken to one's heart and spiritually possessed, like middle-sized and small islands. Man's dream islands, his Utopias, have all been small.

The face of the land

Geologically there are two Jamaicas, one older than the other. The

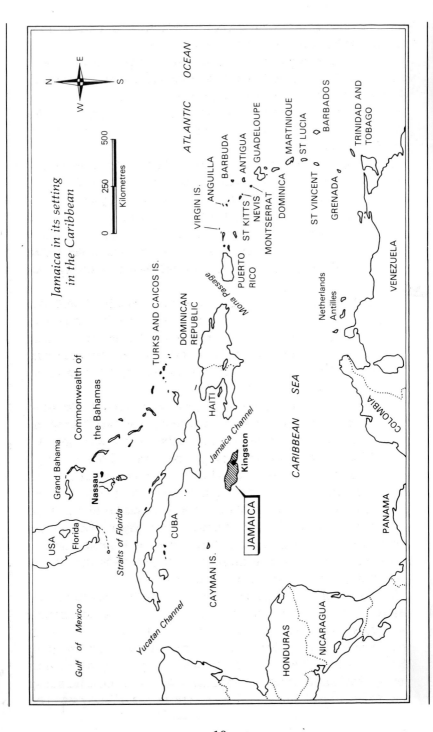

Jamaica in its setting
in the Caribbean

older part is the eastern quarter of the island, which includes the parishes of Portland, St Thomas and St Andrew.

In the far distant past volcanic upheavals thrust this part above sea-level and, after a period of time, submerged it again. Through long ages marine polyps covered it with a blanket of limestone. There followed a series of upheavals which lifted a larger Jamaica above sea-level, with 3000 square miles of limestone-covered rock attached to the older portion.

This second series of upheavals propelled the land upward in stages, forming terraces and plateaux that range from 1500 to 3500 feet above sea-level. Some of the escarpments are spectacular. At Lovers Leap, west of Alligator Pond on the south coast, the land rises abruptly 1600 feet above the sea. On the north coast, inland from Ocho Rios, is the famous Fern Gully, a three-mile water course that runs from the plateau around Hopewell down the escarpment to the coast.

Its thick limestone blanket gave Jamaica its bauxite. Water that contains even a weak solution of acids can dissolve limestone. Through countless millennia the rain dissolved vast quantities of the limestone, leaving the 'red earth' that is so characteristic of central and western Jamaica. The red earth contains iron and bauxite, the ore from which aluminium is made.

Water, a persistent sculptor, wrought other marvels. It produced the Cave River and Hectors River, which rise and then disappear, and the Y.S. River which disappears and then reappears to join the Black River in St Elizabeth. It gouged out sink holes and carved underground channels through which hidden streams drain away into deep lagoons, such as the lagoon at the Green Grotto on the road from Discovery Bay to Runaway Bay. It fashioned a maze of subterranean reservoirs and tunnels, with lakes that appear periodically at Moneague and at Newmarket in Westmoreland. It hollowed out caves such as those in the Dry Harbour mountains, and on the Hopewell and Cave Valley estates.

In a display of power, nature created the almost impenetrable confusion of the Cockpit Country and the John Crow mountains. Describing these mountains that break the power of the north-east trade winds on the Portland coast, the Jamaican novelist, John Hearne, writes: 'There are areas known in any one generation to perhaps half a dozen men . . . In some parts a man could fall a long way down the sink-hole . . . If you move a yard off the paths you

need a machine, and trying to cut your way through a tangle of fairy bamboo makes as much sense as running into a barbed wire fence . . .'

Underground streams and subterranean reservoirs mean a lack of surface water. Jamaicans have found ways of surviving through humdrum routines. In the pastures they have made circular dew-ponds which have provided the cattle with water save in times of extreme drought. As a necessary part of each cottage and house they have built tanks and erected make-shift cisterns for storing water. If the standpipe that brought water from the large public tanks was far away, women and children carried buckets and tins of water on their heads to their homes.

An island of contrasts

Jamaica is an island of contrasts packed close in a small space. Wet Jamaica is in the north-east, the area of the John Crow mountains and the Blue Mountain range. Kenneth Pringle, in a forgotten book, *Waters of the West*, describes what this part of mountain Jamaica is like.

> *The part allotted to Corbett and myself was to proceed up to the Corn Puss Gap and build a hut for the first night's camp. The four foot track wound deviously about the hills above the Rio Grande which all the way sounded louder as it narrowed . . . The Corn Puss Gap is so called, according to the bushmen, because the Maroons once salted (corned) a wild cat in that pass . . .*
>
> *From a flat grass piece just above the knoll you can see north over the dark green irregular ranges as far as the blue arc of water which is Port Antonio and south over the culti-vated mellow plains of St Thomas to the coast at Morant Bay.*
>
> *We built there a tall hut flanked with poles and provided with a raised floor of poles. We wove a fresh green roof of thatch-palm pleated so close that rain could not penetrate. Then we lit a fire under another shelter outside and prepared*

Under the banyan tree *opposite* [JAMAICA TOURIST BOARD, KINGSTON]

*an evening meal of fried mullet and coco and a great shut-
pan of tea. Murray and Jackson and Johnson arrived in time
to smell it and ascend with joyous cries. The bushmen were
in high spirits because of the remarkably fine weather –
'Backra luck' they called it. But Backra's luck did not hold
for long.*

*Sunset that evening was the first sign we had of trouble.
The John Crows, rising sheer above us, vanished in a sombre
watery purple haze. The voices of those a few feet away
sounded like voices heard under water. If one went out, one
was soaked with damp in a few minutes. Yet when we turned
in, it had not yet begun to rain. It started about midnight,
quietly, a long sigh like the breaking of a wave, and streamed
down in a steady sheet. It did not stop, although it lightened
from time to time, for four days.*

This is old Jamaica, one which Jamaicans and their guests will wish
to explore. There the environment has hardly been disturbed. Yet
this was never our environment, for we are imported people living in
a largely imported environment. In this respect we are like many
other New World people. As the population grew the fields and
plantations spread, destroying the natural vegetation. This meant the
disappearance of indigenous animals like the iguana and the Indian
cony, which was 'of a distasteful shape like an overgrown rat'.

Some of the old forest trees remain; mahogany, cedar, bulletwood
which blunts the sharpest nail, mahoe; but they are now sadly
diminished. The imported plants flourish as if this has always been
their home.

The importation of plants started when Arawak Indians from the
basin of the Orinoco began settling in the Caribbean islands six or
seven hundred years after the birth of Christ. They took with them
their basic crops, cassava and maize, their sacred tobacco, and
possibly other plants such as pineapples and sour-sop. But they were
not meat-eaters. They lived off fish and shellfish. The rubbish heaps
outside their village sites showed that they consumed large quantities
of molluscs.

The second wave of importation started with the Spanish settlement of the island in 1500. What a whirlwind of change it was,

Goats: 'the short and simple animals of the poor' [CAROLINE LEE]

produced by a new technology based on steel, gunpowder, the compass, quadrant and sails. The importations included sugar-cane, citrus, cattle, swine and horses. Within the space of a century and a half the Arawaks were swept away by this hurricane.

The third great wave of importation of plants started in the late eighteenth century when the slave population of the sugar islands, Jamaica, Barbados, Antigua and St Kitts, was being wiped out by famine. This was the period of Bligh, the mutiny on the *Bounty* and the arrival in Jamaica of Bligh's second ship, the *Providence*, with seven hundred breadfruit trees and many other plants; the time of Dr Clarke, first government botanist, who brought in the ackee tree from West Africa in 1778; the time of Admiral Rodney and Captain Marshall who captured a French ship taking mango plants from Mauritius to the West Indies in 1782 and had the plants re-routed to Jamaica; and the time of a host of other introductions, such as yams, okra, coffee and guinea grass from Africa.

With the food-bearing trees came also some of the chief flowering trees and shrubs of Jamaica; the allamanda, bougainvillaea, oleander, spathodea and royal poinciana or flamboyant.

No wild animals

Jamaica has no wild animals – no jaguars, pumas, no poisonous snakes. The yellow snake, which was harmless, has disappeared. The mongoose helped to wipe it out, so now the only wild animal the visitor is likely to see is the mongoose himself – crossing a country road, thin, tawny, furtive as a weasel. The lizards are small and harmless, though most Jamaicans recoil from them as from a fierce dragon. The green lizards overcome the colour problem by changing from emerald green to near black, as circumstances require. When courting, the male blows out a splendidly-coloured throat-fan, lemon-yellow, brown, orange, his silent rendering of the wolf-whistle. Quite harmless, but most disliked of all, is the 'croaking lizard' which gets its name from the noise it makes. The folk say, 'When croakin' lizard bawl, sign of rain comin'.'

The birds of Jamaica

Look out for the flying jewels that we call humming birds. There are four varieties in the island: a Mango Hummer, known in Haiti as 'black magic' because a dried powder from its body is an effective love potion: the minute Bee Hummer, of dark green; the Vervain, one of the world's smallest birds; and the Doctor, known also as Streamer-Tail, Long-Tail or Scissors-Tail. The male is a glittering green with the top of the head and crest black. This 'black top hat' earns the bird his name, because in earlier years a doctor's professional dress included a black top hat. The elongated tail feathers of the male form a lovely pair of streamers, often twice the length of the body. The wing and under-tail coverts appear deep violet or blue-black. This hummer, which is found only in the island, is depicted on the Jamaica dollar bill as the national bird.

The Mocking Bird or **Jamaica Nightingale** delights in singing from the topmost twig of a tall tree in the morning and at sunset. He sings at all seasons and, because he seems at times to imitate the notes of other birds, he is called the Mocking Bird. Gosse, in his classic study of the *Birds of Jamaica*, described him as 'bold and forward in his manners, inviting rather than avoiding notice, of striking though not showy colours'. The colouring is silver-grey,

The Jamaican Parrot [CAROLINE LEE]

with large white wing patches and with the outermost feathers of the wing white.

The Jamaica Canary is a finch of the same family as the many quits that feed on the lawns and are prepared to join a visitor at the breakfast table. But he is much more vivid than the Black-face and Yellow-face Grass Quits, more jewel-like even than the Orange Quit or 'Long mout Quit' with its breast of deep chestnut red and (if a male) with violet-blue colouring. The upper parts are a bright olive-yellow, the forehead and crown a bright orange, the underparts a bright yellow. The bill is dull yellow with a dark tip on the lower mandible; altogether an enchanting little bird.

The John Crow is one of the first birds you will see, its plumage black as a parson's coat. It is an expert glider and most graceful in flight, but downright repulsive on land with its funereal appearance and bald red head. It is said that an Irish parson, the Reverend John Crow, preached a very unpopular sermon in Port Royal in the early buccaneering days. The bird's appearance reminded his audience of the priest so they gave it his name in derision. It is a good story but not supported by any evidence. Occasionally there is an albino John Crow; he is known as John Crow Parson or John Crow Headman, being white. There is a Jamaican proverb that warns 'Every John Crow thinks his pickney white' or, your own children (or other possessions) are the best in the world.

The Petchary, small bird of the tyrant flycatcher family, gets his name from his fierce, ceaseless shrieks. If you see a little ball of grey feathers shrieking 'pecheery-pecheery-pecheery' and dive-bombing a John Crow, you will know that you are looking at a petchary. He usually arrives in the island in May.

The Banana Quit, on the other hand, is prepared to share breakfast with you. In Jamaica he has several names – Beany Bird, Bessie Coban and John Croppie. He loves sugar and bananas. Offer him some and he will make himself at home on your table, sometimes too much so. There are a number of other quits, one of the most common being the Grass Quit, a counterpart of the Jamaica Sparrow for cheekiness.

Commonly seen also are the Hopping Dick, or Jumping Dick, a thrush which hops and jumps his way across the garden, and the Ground Doves that feed on the ground. They are safe from boys with sling shots, because to shoot a 'duppy bird' brings disaster, even death. 'Duppy' is Jamaican for 'jumbie' or 'ghost'.

The Rocklands Bird Sanctuary at Anchovy in the hills above Montego Bay should be high on any list of places to be visited in Jamaica.

| 3 |
The Jamaica story

Arawak Jamaica (700 AD to 1600 AD)

What happened to the Arawaks, who discovered the island centuries before Columbus and made it their homeland? Who were they and why are they nowhere to be seen?

The Arawaks were Amerindians from the region of the Orinoco, where their kinsfolk survive to this day. Using dug-out canoes some migrated from the islands and slowly made their way up the islands, taking their food plants with them. Columbus described them in his *Journal:*

> *They all go naked as their mothers bore them, and the women also, although I saw only one very young girl . . .*
>
> *They were very well built, with very handsome bodies and very good faces. Their hair is coarse almost like the hair of a horse's tail and short . . . Some of them are painted black, and they are the colour of the people of the Canaries, neither black nor white . . .*
>
> *They do not bear arms nor know them, for I showed to them swords and they took them by the blade and cut themselves through ignorance . . . Their spears are certain reeds, without iron and some of these have a fish tooth at the end . . .*
>
> *They came to the ship in boats, which are made of a tree-trunk like a long boat and all of one piece. They are wonderfully carved . . . They row them with a paddle . . . and they travel wonderfully fast . . .*

The Arawaks slowly made their way up the line of islands, carrying with them such plants as cassava, sweet potatoes, maize and tobacco, and fruits such as guavas, naseberries or sapodillas, pineapples, sweet sops, sour sops and cashews. They travelled with hammocks, the best portable bed ever made, and they left behind words like hurricane, barbecue, cannibal and maize.

By the time that Columbus arrived there were about 100 000 Arawaks in Jamaica, living along the north and south coasts on hills overlooking the sea from which they gathered the molluscs they loved. The iron-age Europeans, with swords and cannon, wind-propelled ships, horses and cattle, dogs and swine, burst upon these stone-age people like a hurricane. Their diseases wiped out a people without immunity to them. So did cruel enslavement. Jamaica's Arawaks perished within a century and a half after Columbus discovered the island in 1494.

Spanish Jamaica

The Spaniard also is missing. He is present in Puerto Rico, the Dominican Republic and Cuba but not in Jamaica, where he ruled for 150 years, from 1500 to 1655.

The story of Spanish Jamaica began in May 1494 when Columbus, approaching from the north-east, saw the Blue Mountain range pencilled against the sky. Excited, he wrote, 'It is the fairest isle that ever eyes beheld . . . and the mountains seem to touch the sky.' Columbus put in at St Ann's Bay, then sailed west along the coast to Montego Bay which he called 'Bay of Good Weather'. He then sailed back to Cuba. Later that year he rounded Negril and explored part of the south coast.

Nine years later, bad weather forced Columbus, on his way back from Central America, to beach his two badly leaking ships in St Ann's Bay, where he was marooned for a year. We tell the story of Columbus' adventures when we visit St Ann's Bay and Seville.

After Columbus died, his son Diego Colon was appointed Governor of Jamaica. In 1510 his representative Juan de Esquivel established a town, New Seville, near St Ann's Bay. The settlement did not prosper, so twenty-four years later the colonists founded a new capital at St Jago de la Vega, our Spanish Town. Later, small settlements were established at Oristan (Bluefields), and Esquivel (near Old Harbour).

Those were the magic years when Cortes overthrew the Aztec empire in Mexico, when Pizarro conquered Peru with a handful of Conquistadors, and silver, precious stones and gold drew Spanish colonists from the islands like a magnet. 'May God send me to Peru' was their prayer. Only those who were content with ranching, and selling hides, barbecued meat and cassava bread to passing ships stayed in Jamaica.

A lack-lustre period followed, without colour or spectacular events, but the significant often wears drab clothes. Quietly the nondescript colonists gave Jamaica its great crops, oranges, lemons, plantains, bananas and, most important of all, the sugar-cane and the technology for small-scale sugar production, based on wooden mills turned by mules. The story of sugar was to become a continuous thread running through the whole of Caribbean history. The Spanish settlers rounded up the cattle and horses occasionally for branding but, as in Hispaniola, many animals escaped into the forests and mountains. To these runaway animals the Spanish settlers gave the name *cimarones* from *cima*, peak. Later, any runaway was called a 'maroon'.

The importations greatly enlarged the food-supply inherited from the Arawaks and, in time, transformed the landscape. Most significant of all, the settlers brought their African slaves with them. By 1655 there were about 1500 of them, roughly one-half the population of the island.

The English capture Jamaica (1655)

An English expeditionary force, sent out by Cromwell to break Spain's hold on the Caribbean, after being driven off from Santo Domingo, and being terrified of returning empty-handed to Cromwell, captured weakly-held Jamaica in May 1655. The feeble, ageing Governor and most of the colonists left for Cuba, except for a small company of resolute men who held parts of the north coast for five years. The Africans, free and left to fend for themselves, formed three bands under elected leaders and set up mountain bases from which they waged guerilla war against the English. The best known of their leaders, Lubola, who worked in concert with Yssassi, providing him with food and information, finally accepted an English offer of peace – one not easily rejected since an English officer had discovered the Maroon leader's food base of 200 acres at Lluidas Vale. Lubola dared not risk its destruction. In return for the recognition of their freedom and their right of self-government Lubola agreed to keep the peace and to refrain from assisting Yssassi, who was defeated by the English.

In this way Jamaica became a British Colony. It remained so for 300 years, up to 1962 when it became independent.

The Age of the Buccaneers

The name 'buccaneer' comes from the word 'boucan', the process of curing strips of meat by smoking them over a slow fire. The *boucaniers* were originally men who lived by hunting and by selling hides and smoked meat to passing ships. These masterless men, runaways, felons, marooned or ship-wrecked sailors, often varied hunting with robbery by land or sea. They formed the nucleus of the bands of pirates who established bases at Tortuga and Port Royal and, in times of war, served the British, French and Dutch as commando forces against the Spanish.

English buccaneers began to make their headquarters at Port Royal soon after the British took Jamaica from Spain. Within ten years there emerged a leader, Henry Morgan, who came out to Barbados as an indentured servant and ran away to join the buccaneers. He rose to power and, in the 1660s and early 1670s reached the height of his fame. In the taverns of Port Royal cut-throats and daredevils told how Morgan raided the Spanish town of Porto Bello, tortured and killed those who lived there and returned to Port Royal with 300 000 silver 'pieces of eight'. They told of Morgan's raid on Maracaibo and of the 250 000 pieces of eight he brought back. They

Pewter [HERBIE GORDON]

gloried most of all in his bloodiest triumph, the capture and destruction of Panama.

The Treaty of Madrid between Spain and Britain marked the end of the 'Age of the Buccaneers', Britain's abandonment of a policy of pillage and Spain's acknowledgement of the presence of Britain in the Caribbean. Peace with Spain and trade became the goals of British policy.

Sugar islands and Yankee traders

From the 1640s on there was an interweaving of North American and West Indian interests.

William Vassal and Richard Vines transplanted themselves from New England to the West Indies, and became agents for merchant friends in Boston and elsewhere. A two-way movement began, with traders going from the Caribbean to Boston, and numbers of Barbadian planters moving to the Carolinas. The first four governors of the Carolinas were Barbadians. The Winthrops, one of the most influential of the New England families, held trading offices in Rhode Island, Hartford, Barbados and Antigua.

The trade included a wide range of goods. From Jamaica and other West Indian islands the trade was in sugar and molasses and from North America came plantation supplies such as salted fish, wheat, peas, pork, corn, cattle, pipe-staves, clapboards and lumber.

Sightseeing deepens into insight with awareness that Jamaica's Great Houses and sugar estates, the African labour force and North American traders all formed part of a vigorous expanding Atlantic Basin trading area. Awareness of this three hundred years of inter-connectedness explains why Jamaica, though in many ways so different, nevertheless has the appeal of the familiar.

Sugar was to the seventeenth and eighteenth centuries what oil is to our century. Like a powerful magnet it brought traders crowding into the Caribbean each year from the ports of Western Europe and North America. Sugar set the fleets and armies of Europe grappling with each other. Sugar made the plantation islands more valuable parts of the British empire than was New England. It induced France to yield the whole continent of North America east of the Mississippi to Britain for the return of Guadeloupe and Martinique. It produced the wealth that dazzled Britain. It produced the money that financed the industrial revolution in Britain and in France, and it enabled the West Indian interest to control so many seats in the House of Commons and to gain so much political power that Benjamin Franklin confessed they far outweighed the Northern colonies.

That was one side of the story. The wealth flowed from large plantations manned by black labour. In the course of three hundred and fifty years sugar brought more than ten million blacks from West Africa to the New World. Throughout the islands and in north-east Brazil the unit of production was the same, the sugar and slave plantation.

The growth of the industry was much more than the spread of a profitable crop. It changed the racial composition and social structure of the islands. It resulted in the spread of large estates wherever sugar could be grown, with ownership in the hands of a small number of white owners, many of whom lived in England; in the importation of large numbers of Africans, so that by the end of the eighteenth century blacks in Jamaica outnumbered whites by ten to one. It meant also a regime of exploitation of both labourer and land, and it was supported by a system of discrimination based on skin colour.

Two Jamaicas

Two Jamaicas came into existence, with two sets of people who lived in the same island, were engaged in producing one crop, but who lived in worlds that were very different. The layout of the plantations mirrored the differences, with Great House and slave huts, fields of sugar-cane on the fertile lowlands and the provision grounds of the blacks on marginal land. Both societies were profoundly affected by the same moulding forces. Colonialism bred habits of dependence and of reliance on some external authority. The system of slavery engendered attitudes of superiority among whites and of inferiority among blacks. The plantation system, as it was managed, led to the destruction of natural resources. Because the economic and social system was restrictive, it created counter-movements, the 'haves' resisting change, and the 'have-nots' struggling for change.

Black protest took many forms: sabotage and 'go-slows' on the plantations, malingering and the like; running away, mutinies and rebellion. In Jamaica no African name sounded more clearly than those of Ashanti and Coromanti. 'These,' reported a West Indian planter, 'were accustomed to war from infancy, were energetic of mind, hardy and robust, but bringing with them into slavery lofty ideas of independence, they are dangerous inmates of a West Indian plantation.' Codrington, Governor of the Leeward Islands, spoke of them as not only the best and most faithful of the slaves, 'but [they] are really all born heroes. There never was a rascal or coward of that region.' The will for change, the capacity for leadership and the dynamism were rooted in the mass of the people.

Rise of a peasantry

The next climactic event was the emancipation of all slaves in the British Empire, in 1834. The slave was no longer another man's property. He was free to sell his labour to the estate or to withold it. Ten years later, the British Parliament established free trade and removed the preferential tariff on West Indian sugar. Emancipation and free trade destroyed the old slave-and-sugar plantation. The Jamaican people set about building homes and free villages often with the help and guidance of Baptist and Methodist missionaries. William Knibb, who had fiercely opposed slavery and had championed the cause of emancipation, wrote: 'By the census taken during last year I find that there were full 19 000 persons, formerly slaves, who had purchased land on which they were erecting their own cottages.' Most countries start with a peasantry. Jamaica started late, but in the years between 1834 and 1850 a black peasantry emerged.

The old representative system remained. It was in fact an oligarchy, political power resting in the hands of a small group of planters and merchants. In 1865, following a rising of black peasants in Morant Bay, the House of Assembly surrendered its powers and Jamaica was ruled by a governor who represented the British sovereign. The small class which had ruled Jamaica since 1660, when the sytstem of representative government was introduced, lost much of its power. It retained considerable influence, however, and, since the franchise for elections to the Legislative Council was restricted, it kept its place as part of the political system. The great mass of the people were excluded. The two Jamaicas remained, divided by colour and ethnic origin. The old plantation system had been destroyed but the attitudes it had engendered still divided the society. The power of the plantocracy had been greatly diminished but the élite jealously guarded its preserves. On the other hand colonialism had been strengthened, and the society remained essentially conservative. The social structure remained that of a pyramid, with a small élite of white and brown at the top, a larger middle layer of brown and a few black middle-class people, and a large base of black peasants.

The dynamism was in the base. By 1860, less than thirty years after emancipation, Jamaica had more than 50 000 holdings of under fifty acres each. By 1900 the number had risen to 130 000. The number of holdings in the five to fifty acre range increased. There was a shift from provision grounds to mixed farming, combining ground provisions for the domestic market with export crops such as ginger, bananas, coconuts and logwood. In 1850 the produce of the Jamaican peasantry was about eighty-three per cent ground provisions and about eleven per cent export crops. In 1890 the percentage of export crops was twenty-three. Reviewing this record, a Royal Commission which visited Jamaica in 1897 pointed out that the peasantry were a source of economic and political strength.

By 1920 there were several critical issues for Jamaica. Could racial discrimination be brought to an end? Could Jamaica produce leaders who would build a spirit of national unity? Could these leaders bring all Jamaicans into the political system and put their future in their hands?

The answers were given by leaders who emerged from among the people and who had full popular support. Outstanding among them were Alexander Bustamante and Norman Manley, two of Jamaica's national heroes and the architects of her independence.

Alexander Bustamante

Alexander Bustamante was born in 1884 of a lower middle-class family of very limited means. He was an extrovert with a remarkable zest for life and a delight in people. He left Jamaica when he was twenty, travelled widely in Cuba, Panama, the United States and Spain, came back to Jamaica at the age of fifty, and soon attracted attention by his championship of the masses and his attacks on the privileged and powerful. He founded the Bustamante Industrial Trade Union, became the acknowledged labour leader of Jamaica, was charged with sedition and thrown into detention camp in 1942. He was released later in 1942, founded the Jamaica Labour Party, swept to power in the elections of 1944, and thereafter for thirty years dominated Jamaican politics.

'Busta' was the kind of man around whom legends gather. He was six feet two inches in height, bony and angular in the style of Abraham Lincoln with a great shock of hair and long arms that appeared to be telescopic; when he was gesturing with them in front of a crowd they seemed to grow longer and longer.

We can form an impression of 'Busta' or 'The Chief' as a person by looking at him through the eyes of a cub reporter of the time, Ulric Simmonds, and of the late Lord Caradon, Governor of Jamaica.

> *I remember how good he was with crowds* [Ulric Simmonds wrote]. *How he could move them, sway them and keep them tightly under control or move them to violent action at other times . . . but no one would touch me because I was with Busta.* [Lord Caradon wrote] *He sometimes appears reckless and irresponsible, or rather he used to in his earlier days, but always he shrewdly calculates the effect of his action . . . we soon discovered when he became Minister that he had an astonishingly quick and sure grasp of administrative problems and a political sense which was almost uncanny.*

A man of great charisma, Busta knew intuitively how to maintain his leadership. He was the dynamite that broke up the traditional barriers of privilege and colour in Jamaica. He saw people and not colour or rank. Light-brown himself, he identified with and was accepted by the predominantly black masses. He shattered the colour bar that had separated Jamaicans for centuries.

Norman Manley

Norman Manley was born in 1894 of a lower middle-class family. He spent his early years on a derelict property which his widowed mother managed.

*The property carried on as best it could with a little of
everything, logwood, a few cattle, a few tenants, a little cocoa.
She made all our clothes, made jellies when guavas were in,
kept a small chicken farm and ran things with firm efficiency.
When night came she disappeared into her own room to write
letters to her few remaining friends, nearly all of whom
deserted her when she married a near-black man . . .*

Manley won a Rhodes scholarship, entered Oxford to study law
and read for the bar, but enlisted in an artillery regiment in World
War I with his brother, Roy, who had been denied a commission
because he was not white. Roy was killed in action. Norman was
awarded the Military Medal for bravery. He returned to Oxford after
the war, was Prizeman at Gray's Inn and took first-class Honours
in his Bar finals. He married his cousin Edna Swithenbank who in
time became Jamaica's most distinguished sculptor, returned to
Jamaica, and soon became the island's foremost lawyer. He became
leader of the emerging national movement and formed the People's
National Party in 1938.

Manley was an introvert who reached his conclusions by analysis.
He recognised Jamaica's need for a vital sustaining principle, 'a spirit
of national unity', and for institutions which expressed and sustained
that spirit. His single most important contribution was ensuring that
the 1944 constitution granted the right to vote to all adult Jamaicans.
Bustamante swept the Jamaican working class into the mainstream
of Jamaican political life and Norman Manley secured the constitutional changes that put political power in their hands.

Although cousins, the two men were very different; extrovert and
introvert, intuitive and analytic, mass orator and advocate, they
complemented each other. They were opponents but never enemies,
adversaries but always Jamaicans. Around them Jamaica's two chief
trade unions and political parties took shape and grew. Their
example of respect for democracy, for Parliament and the Constitution kept the young nation stable and engendered in Jamaicans of
all classes pride and confidence in their country. They did not
generate the spirit of independence. That manifested itself at the
very start of the settlement of Jamaica, with the Maroons and the
slave risings; through the rise of a black peasantry and the dynamism
that sent thousands of Jamaicans overseas in search of larger
opportunities; through the mass acceptance of Garvey; and through

working class struggles and a sophisticated understanding of the political process and of political issues. Independent Jamaica grew out of the spirit of independence of the Jamaican people.

Independent Jamaica

On 6 August, 1962 Jamaica became an independent nation. On that day the Parliament of Jamaica met to receive from HRH Princess Margaret, representing the Queen, the documents that established Jamaica's constitutional standing. The first Prime Minister of the independent country, Alexander Bustamante, received the documents and the leader of the Opposition, Norman Washington Manley, joined in the ceremony, making a three-minute speech that is still remembered as one of the finest he ever made. He affirmed what independence means to Jamaicans everywhere.

We here today stand surrounded by an unseen host of witnesses, the men who in the past and through all our history strove to keep alight the torch of freedom in this country. No one will name them today but this House is in very deed their memorial . . .

And what of the future that lies before us? We have come to independence prepared and ready to shoulder our new responsibilities and united I believe in one single hope that we may make our small country a safe and happy place for all our people . . .

Many of us dare to believe that this country, so blended in origins, so fashioned in time, so wrought on by our own history may go out into the world to make a contribution larger than our size would lead one to expect.

I believe that as an independent nation we can so manage ourselves as to demonstrate how by making our great motto 'Out of many one people' come to speak the truth about ourselves, we can become a worthwhile and shining example of the sort of world men sometimes dream to live in.

You, Princess, have handed us the formal title deeds to our heritage. For us the task is to plough the land and gather the fruit.

The Governor-General opens Parliament (Gordon House)
[JAMAICA INFORMATION SERVICE]

The system of government

Like many other independent countries which were formerly part of the British Empire, Jamaica chose to remain a member of the British Commonwealth, the head of which is the British Sovereign. The Governor-General of Jamaica represents the Sovereign. He is named by the Prime Minister of Jamaica, and then appointed by the Sovereign. The Governor-General has no power but that of veto, and this can only be exercised on the advice of the Cabinet.

Power rests with the party elected to govern the country, normally for a period of five years. All Jamaicans over eighteen years of age have the right to vote. The leader of the party that wins the election is invited by the Governor-General to be Prime Minister and to form a government. The Prime Minister appoints the Ministers of Government. These form the Cabinet, which formulates government policy and proposes it to the House of Representatives.

The legislature consists of two houses, the House of Representatives and the Senate. Members of the House of Representatives are elected, each member representing one of the constituencies into which the island is divided. The House appoints from amongst its members a Chairman, the Speaker, who presides over the meetings of the House and sees that parliamentary procedure is observed.

The Senate is a nominated body. Members are appointed by the Governor-General on the advice of the Prime Minister. The leader of the opposition names a stated number of those to be appointed. The chief function of the Senate is to review legislation sent forward by the elected House.

Law and administration

To safeguard its independence and impartiality the Judiciary is separate from the Legislature. The Chief Justice, Judges of the Supreme Court and of High Courts, judges, magistrates, Justices of the Peace and members of the police force are Jamaicans.

Security is in the hands of the Jamaica police force and the Jamaica Regiment, which consists of men recruited in Jamaica and under the command of Jamaican officers.

Local government is administered by two bodies: elected Councillors of a number of cities or municipalities, each Council having the right to elect a Mayor; and elected members of Parish Councils. Each Parish Council receives grants from the Central Government to assist it in carrying out its business.

The Civil Service administers the business of central Government. In each Ministry there is a Permanent Secretary, a career official who advises the Minister but does not make policy. He is responsible for carrying out decisions taken by the government. The Civil Service has two main branches, the technical and administrative, and the clerical.

Civil servants have permanent full-time appointments. They do not lose their jobs when a new government is elected to power. All matters affecting the service, such as promotions, complaints and training, are dealt with by The Ministry of Public Service.

In addition to the departments in each Ministry there are a number of Statutory Boards which are set up to perform certain specific duties. These include the Jamaica Broadcasting Corporation, Jamaica's Economic Development Agency (JAMPRO) and the Jamaica Tourist Board.

| 4 |
Jamaica's folk-lore, seed-bed of a culture

In the beginning an uprooting

Most North Americans, like West Indians, are imported people, but the North Americans were transplanted whereas the ancestors of all New World blacks were forcibly uprooted. They endured the traumatic shock of an almost total sundering from their roots as well as the formidable task of settling into a strange and often hostile cultural environment.

They had no written records. Their stories, history, music, customs and ancestral beliefs were lodged in their minds. Though they were all Africans, they came from many different tribes and regions, spoke different languages, and held different religious beliefs. Some were from the Wolofs and Mandingoes of Senegambia. Others were from the Denkyera, the Fante, Ashanti and Akim people. Yet others were from Dahomey and others were Yorubas, Ibo, Fon and Edo people. They came from a region as large and as diverse as Western Europe. They were brought as individuals, and it was the policy to keep them apart from their compatriots in order to lessen the danger of their combining to foment uprisings.

Gradually from their accumulated experience the folk began to put down their roots and to create a new way of life, a culture that was their own. How did they do it? The strongest link between them was not that of tribe or family but of having travelled from Africa on the same slave ship; they were not kinsmen, not fellow tribesmen, but shipmates; it was a relationship of chance, not of blood. They did not know it, but they had little time in which to get acquainted; the life expectation of a slave was seven years. The Arawaks had chosen mass suicide. Some of the Africans chose to die; they pined away. But the majority, without planning, as a natural response to this terrible fate, chose to live, to adjust, to put down their roots. Just as technology is man's response to his environment, so the folk culture of the Jamaican and West Indian folk is a record of a people's response

33

Folk dancing [JAMAICA TOURIST BOARD, NEW YORK]

to their new environment. It was a way of meeting their spiritual and psychological needs. The folk, not the governments, not those in authority, established a seed-bed for a national culture; not deliberately, but as part of an agonising process of ensuring that they survived. From this seed-bed has grown a national culture which has ties with other cultures but which is uniquely Jamaican. We can witness this evolution. This is why Jamaica can be a venue for fun and for learning.

Jamaica talk

What language do Jamaicans speak? The best reply is given by a Jamaican scholar, Frederic Cassidy, now in the United States directing a monumental project, a Dictionary of American Regional English (DARE).

What language do Jamaicans talk? The question is asked not only by strangers to the Caribbean but also by English and American visitors who have heard Jamaicans speaking what they did not at first recognize as a type of their own tongue. It is a question raised as well by students of language, and they mean, How is Jamaica Talk to be classified – as a type of English, or as something quite different, though obviously related? A real question, this, which deserves a sound answer – one, however, that cannot be given until we have carefully examined the language as Jamaicans use it.

Another and equally interesting question is, How did Jamaicans come to talk as they do? The musical lilt and staccato rhythms, the mingling of strange words, the vowel sounds that go sliding off into diphthongs, the cheerful defiance of many niceties of traditional English grammar, the salty idioms, the wonderfully compressed proverbs, the pungent imagery of nick-names and epithets in the bestowal of which these islanders appear to be peculiarly adept – where do all these hail from, and how did they come to be? ...

But it is not by peculiarities of vocabulary alone that Jamaica talk is characterised. The pronunciation differs in some striking ways from that of standard English, and in the grammar of the common folk we find the widest differences of all. The first time that an outsider hears spoken Jamaican he will be struck by unfamiliar sounds and rhythms; some words he will recognise fairly soon, others will be new; but hardest to grasp will be the phrases in which – to him – some words are unexpectedly missing and others unexpectedly present. If he concludes that this is a chaotic babble he will be wrong. The rules are different, but he may be assured that there are *rules.*

The tradition is of an oral, not a written language. It expresses the mood of the moment; the speaker uses intonation, repetition, imagery, gesture, filling each word with drama. Lifeless things come to life: I do not drop a cup; the 'wutless something' jump right out of me hand. I do not miss the bus; the bus left me. I do not forget to mail the letter my friend gave me; that letter jus' fly out of me mind. I do not meet a friend; instead I convey the impression of a collision, for 'I buck up with him'.

Irony, satire and ridicule are the dominant characteristics. They are used not only against others but against oneself, to express anxiety, concern or inner doubt. Louise Bennett, in her poem celebrating Jamaica's independence in 1962, caught the mood perfectly.

> *Independence wid a vengeance,*
> *Independence raisin' Cain,*
> *Jamaica start grow beard, ah hope*
> *We chin can stan' de strain.*

Continuing the mood of pride mingled with self-mockery, how will the new nation fare in a world of super-powers armed with atomic bombs?

> *We defence is not defenceless*
> *For we got half-a-brick,*
> *We got we broken bottle*
> *And we Cookomacca stick . . .*

This gift for vivid imagery, so characteristic of West African proverbs, gives Jamaican proverbs the sparkle of sunshine. Instead of the dark sayings of the wise we have the wise sayings of the dark, each a crystallisation of experience in a single image. Thus, 'hard words break no bones' becomes 'Cuss-cuss (abuse) never bore hole in skin'. 'Familiarity breeds contempt' becomes 'If you play with puppy, puppy lick you mouth'. 'Don't play with edged tools' is vivified as 'You never see dawg chaw razor'.

Animals and insects become teachers, warning us against the kind of behaviour that made life difficult for people torn away from a network of tribal and family relationships, powerless against oppression and often short of food. In such circumstances let those in authority remember that when a powerful man falls those who are weak can take advantage of him. 'When cotton-tree fall down even nanny goat jump over him', and 'Every day you goad donkey, one day him will kick you'. The poor dare not show their anger, so 'Poor man never vex'. The powerless should choose their friends with care: 'Not everybody who kin (skins, shows) them teeth wid you is friend'; also, 'Man you can't beat, you have to call him fren''. Be discreet and let the entry of a third person put an end to gossip:

36

'When six yeye (eyes) meet, story done'. Do not mock others, remember that 'Little pig ask him mama (mother) what make her mout' so long, she say "Never mind, me pickney, that same thing that make fe me (mine) long will make fe you (yours) long too".' Poor people who show off should remember that 'When dawg mauger (thin) him head big'. Every man needs help, for 'One finger can't catch dog-flea'. Guard the tongue: 'When you go to donkey house don't talk about ears', and look after your own interests, for 'You can't keep crow from flying but you can keep him from pitching on you' head'.

Anansi stories

The chief character in the folktales of Jamaica is Anansi, often spelled Anancy. The word Ananse, a spider, is from the Twi language of West Africa; it also means Creator because he makes something out of nothing, i.e. his web. He symbolises the triumph of wit over brute strength and, like Proteus, he is able to take many forms. The spider's web was often spoken of as 'Anancy rope'. Sometimes, when old women got sleepy, Anansi tied up their faces with his rope.

The Ashanti people brought their spider-god with them across the Atlantic, and with him came his son Tacooma and his wife Crooky. The uprooted people kept alive the West African tradition of story-telling, in which the story-teller dramatised the tale, with Anansi changing from spider to man,

Ticky-Picky Boom-Boom

At last the famine was over. The rains came. First heavy black clouds covered the sky, and then the rain came down in floods. The dry earth seemed to drink up the rain until it could drink no more. The parched brown grass became green. Life started again, and everyone began to plant.

Even Anansi set to work. Never before had he worked so hard or so long. At last the large square of land round his

---

Junkanoo dancers *overleaf* [JAMAICA TOURIST BOARD, KINGSTON]

house was full of yams and potatoes.

Now the yams were ready. Anansi looked out from his window at the field of yams and said to himself: 'I must have a garden with flowers in it, like a rich man. I will get Tiger to come and dig up the yams for me.'

Anansi went to Tiger and said: 'Good morning, Mr Tiger. I hope you are very well. I beg you to come with your hoe and machete and dig my yams.'

'What will you give me?' asked Tiger, stroking his moustache and looking hard at Anansi. He was beginning to be a little suspicious of this Anansi, who always got the better of him.

'I will give you all the yams that you dig up,' said Anansi.

That was fair enough, thought greedy Mr Tiger. Next morning he went to Mr Anansi's house early with his hoe and machete; and he dug and dug; and the more he dug, the more the yams seemed to grow down into the ground. By and by four o'clock came, working time was over, and Tiger had not dug up a single yam.

Tiger was angry. He looked at the yams and the deep holes that he had dug round them, and he thought of how hard and long he had worked, and he could keep his temper no longer. Tiger took his machete and chopped at one of the yams with it. He chopped into little pieces as much of the yam as he could reach, and then he set off for home.

What was that? There was a noise behind him. Tiger looked round, and he saw all the yams coming after him.

Some of the yams had one leg, some had two legs, some had three legs, some had four legs.

And the noise that their feet made as they came stamping and running down the road sounded like this:

"Ticky-Picky Boom-Boom,
Ticky-Picky Boom-Boom, Boof!'

Tiger began to run. The yams ran, too. Tiger began to gallop. The yams galloped, too. Tiger jumped. The yams jumped. Tiger made for Brother Dog's house as fast as he could, and he called out at the top of his voice:

'Oh, Brother Dog, Brother Dog, hide me from the yams.'

Dog said, 'All right, Tiger, hide behind me and don't say a word.'

So Tiger hid behind Dog.

Down the road came the yams, stamping on their two legs, three legs, four legs:

'Ticky-Picky, Boom-Boom,
Ticky-Picky Boom-Boom, Boof!'

And they said, 'Brother Dog, did Tiger go this way?'

Mr Dog looked straight ahead and said: 'You know, Mr Yam, I can't see Mr Tiger at all.'

But Tiger could not keep still. He was so frightened that he called out, 'Don't tell them, Mr Dog!' And Mr Dog was so angry that he ran away and left Tiger.

And the yams jumped.

And Tiger jumped.

And the yams ran, and Tiger ran.

The yams galloped, and Tiger galloped.

Then Tiger saw Sister Duck and all her little ducklings by the side of the river. Tiger hurried to her as fast as he could and cried, 'Sister Duck, hide me, hide me from the yams that are coming.'

'All right, Tiger,' she said. 'Get behind me, but don't say a word.'

So Tiger hid behind Sister Duck.

By and by the yams came stamping along.

'Ticky-Picky Boom-Boom,
Ticky-Picky Boom-Boom, Boof!'

And the yams said: 'Sister Duck, have you seen Tiger?'

Sister Duck looked straight ahead and said: 'I can't see him, Yams, I can't see him at all.'

But Tiger was so frightened that he called out, 'Don't tell them, Sister Duck, don't tell them!' And Sister Duck was so angry that she moved away and left him to the yams.

And the yams jumped, and Tiger jumped.

And the yams ran, and Tiger ran.

And the yams galloped, and Tiger galloped.

Tiger was growing tired. Always he could hear the yams coming behind him. At last he came to a little stream, and over it there was a plank of wood. On the other side was Mr Goat.

Tiger ran across the plank as fast as he could and he cried: 'Oh, my Brother Goat, hide me from the yams that are coming.'

'All right, Tiger, but you must not say a word.'

So Tiger hid behind Goat.

The yams came stamping down the road:

'Ticky-Picky Boom-Boom,
Ticky-Picky Boom-Boom, Boof!'

When they reached the little bridge they called out, 'Mr Goat, have you seen Tiger?'

Mr Goat looked straight ahead, but before he could say a word Tiger called out, 'Don't tell them, Mr Goat, don't tell them!'

The yams jumped on to the wooden plank and tried to cross; but Goat put his head down and butted them, one after another, so that they all fell down into the river and were broken in pieces.

Brother Tiger and Brother Goat picked up all the pieces and
went off to Tiger's home to have a great feast.
And they never asked Anansi to the feast of yams.
And sometimes, when the night is dark, Tiger still feels
frightened when he hears someone stamping down the forest
track with a noise that sounds like:
　　　　'Ticky-Picky Boom-Boom,
　　　　Ticky-Picky Boom-Boom, Boof!'

Folk-songs and spirituals

One of the best known of the folk-songs tells of a woman at Linstead
market at evening time, the mangoes in her basket unsold, her
children hungry at home. Those who passed by took up the
mangoes, felt them to see if they were ripe, and went away without
buying even a quattie (3 cents) worth. The woman sings sadly:

'Carry me ackee go a Linstead market,
Not a quattie worth sell,
Carry me ackee go a Linstead market,
Not a quattie worth sell,
Lord, what a night, not a bite,
What a Saturday night,
Everybody come feel-up, feel-up
Not a quattie worth sell . . . '

Perhaps the loveliest of these songs is 'Day dah light' (the day is
dawning). It was sung by women who had been working on the
wharf all night, loading a waiting ship with bananas, each carrying
a heavy bunch on her head at the double, then hurrying back for
another bunch; at last daybreak comes and the run slows to a walk.
They call out to the tally-man who has kept count of the bananas
they carried and the money they earned, and sing:

'Day oh, day oh,
Day dah light an' me wan' fe go home,
Day oh, day oh,
Day dah light an' me wan' fe go home,
Come Mr Tallyman, come tally me banana,
Day dah light an' me wan' fe go home.

Jamaican folk singers [JAMAICA TOURIST BOARD, KINGSTON]

Some songs ridicule failings and follies, as in the picture of a man who, years ago, went off to Colon to work on the Panama Canal. He made money and came back with a fine suit, complete with waist-coat and a watch, the chain of which he wore in the fashionable way, across his stomach. But he was not able to read. He still told the time by the sun:

> '*One, two, three, four, Colon man dah come,*
> *One, two, three, four, Colon man dah come,*
> *Brass chain dah lick him belly bam, bam bam,*
> *You ask him for the time*
> *Him look upon de sun ...*'

Much more shattering is the mockery of a woman abandoned by her soldier lover while she is expecting their child:

> '*What's de use of you shawl-up, shawl-up*
> *Gal, you character gone,*
> *What's de use of you lace-up, stays-up*
> *What's de use of you lace-up, stays-up*
> *Gal, you character gone ...*'

The Jamaica spirituals and revivalist songs have a haunting beauty. Olive Lewin, Founder and Director of the Jamaica Folk Singers, a distinguished group of Jamaican singers, has pioneered the collection and presentation of these songs. In her collection there is a moving song about a gathering in heaven.

'Who will go and die for Adam, . . .
When the question was asked in heaven
There was half an hour silence
There was half an hour silence
Who will go and die for Adam?
I will go,
I will go.'

There is a lovely song about Mary:

'Although the road be rocky and steep
I ask my Saviour to be my guide,
And when I turn my eyes up to heaven
I saw Mary at her Master feet . . .'

Jamaicans are deeply religious in more than a church-going sense. There are the services on Sunday and there are cults and 'revivalists', people who seek 'to live right'; memorial dances to put the dead at rest; white-robed sisters bending and swaying to the hypnotic rhythm of hand-clapping and the tapping of feet; a belief in a spirit world and in life after death. The spirit world is not remote or separate from the world of the living, but forms a unity with it.

| 5 |
Culture, sport and related activities

Caribbean creativity

The population of the English-speaking Caribbean numbers six million. Their record of creativity, in relation to the size of population is astonishing: a Nobel prize winner in economics; internationally acclaimed writers such as Vidia Naipaul, George Lamming and Derek Walcott; world-famous singers such as Sparrow, Bob Marley and his son, Ziggy; uniquely different forms of music such as reggae and the steel band; one of the finest cricket teams in the world; some of the world's fastest runners and women of great charm and beauty who from time to time take the world titles in beauty contests.

Jamaica's culture – including sport – is in a period of great flowering. It is a culture with a unique quality because it has its roots deep in the indigenous, deep in the Jamaican way of life. Let us keep company briefly with some of those who helped to build a culture with a life and vitality of its own.

The Rastafarian contribution

The Ras Tafari movement began to take shape in the 1930s, a decade in which social discontent erupted in a series of volcanic explosions throughout the archipelago, from Cuba to Trinidad and beyond to Guyana. The causes were widespread unemployment, frustration at being doomed to squalor and anger at being rejected by those in power in the society and by those who were better off and better educated. The anger was intensified by Mussolini's attack on Ethiopia, another example of white oppression of blacks.

Groups of Rastafarians emerged in the slums of West Kingston. Having been rejected by the white world, they in their turn rejected all forms of white power and rule, including the Christian Church.

Jamaica was Babylon, Hell, and there was no hope for it. They echoed Marcus Garvey's demand for a return to the homeland, Africa. They based their teaching on the Old Testament and the Book of Revelation. They worshipped a black God, Haile Selassie, Emperor of Ethiopia. They believed that they were the re-incarnation of the ancient Israelites, and that they had been exiled to the West Indies for their transgressions. They believed also that, just as the scattered tribes of Israel had been redeemed and brought back from Babylon, so they would be redeemed and taken back to Africa. They were sons of the mighty God, Jah. Each son of Jah has direct contact with the Father. No son of Jah dies. At the heart of their religious system is the notion of their divinity and 'the first-person image of self'. Those who had been rejected, who had been outcasts in the society, became in their eyes the centre of the Cosmos. There are variations of style and differences of doctrine. Some Rastas wear dreadlocks, following the prohibition in the Book of Leviticus against shaving the hair. Others are bald-headed. Some are poor, from the masses. Others are from middle-class homes. They reject the traditional West Indian values and the existing social structure. Whether the doctrines are true or false, and however bizarre they might seem, Rastafarianism gave to the Brethren a sense of identity, of personal worth, of purpose, of a future.

This affirmation of identity expresses itself in a refusal to use the personal pronoun 'me' which is a mark of subservience, of acceptance of the role of being an 'object'. A Rastafarian uses the pronoun 'I', the plural of which is 'I-and-I' or 'I-n-I'. The reflexive is 'I-self' or 'I-n-I self'. Using this form, the words of Jesus, 'I testify on my own behalf and the Father who sent me . . .' becomes 'I testify on I own behalf and the Father who sent I . . .'

Ganja, *Cannabis sativa*, is a sacred herb for all Rastafarians. They speak of it as 'wisdom weed' or the 'holy weed'. 'The chalice' or 'cup' is the pipe used for smoking the weed. They testify also to its healing power. You can drink it as a tea, or rub your skin with the ashes, or smoke it; and the Lord God is a smoker, for in the book of Genesis we read that 'God says, Behold, I have given you every herb bearing seed, which is upon the face of the earth' . . . and Psalm 18 tells how 'There went up a smoke out of his (The Lord's) nostrils, and fire out of his mouth devoured; the coals were kindled by it.'

Rastafarians defend their use of ganja by insisting on the 'weed's' sacred character, and by attacking the double standards that prevail

47

Kapo [JAMAICA TOURIST BOARD, KINGSTON]

in Babylon, which permits the use of alcohol and tobacco. The use of ganja is the central point of conflict between the Rastas and the Government of Jamaica.

The movement has changed greatly since the early days of police harassment and public contempt. There are now rich Rastas as well as poor; influential and internationally known Rastas as well as obscure Brethren. These changes will raise problems for the followers of Ras Tafari. There is no doubt, however, that the discovery of identity and personal worth has profoundly influenced the cultural and social development of Jamaica. A great flood of creative energy has been released. Painters are producing work of great beauty and power. So are the sculptors. Names to bear in mind are Dunkley, Everald Brown, Kapo. These are among the leading 'intuitives', a term applied by David Boxer, Director of the National Gallery, and other Jamaican critics to those artists whose vision is pure and sincere. 'They are for the most part self-taught. Their visions (and many are true visionaries) as released through canvas or wood are unmediated expressions of their individual relationships with the world around them, and the world within.' Boxer,

Rastafarian Brothers *(opposite)* [JAMAICA TOURIST BOARD, KINGSTON]

49

in a catalogue of the first exhibition of Jamaican Intuitive art, emphasised that 'a stream emerges, a school if you will, that rivals, and for me outshines the other great Caribbean outpouring of "primitive" art, the Haitian school.'

Music also became a medium through which Bob Marley, the Reggae Band, Third World, Burning Spear, Peter Tosh, Jimmy Cliff, Dennis Brown and others voiced a message against injustice, and gave comfort to the oppressed. As Bob Marley sang:

Fly away home to Zion, fly away home,
One bright morning when my work is over
I will fly away home . . .

Keeping company with Jamaica involves understanding that 'Fly away home to Zion' is not a fancy phrase but reality. It means bearing in mind the words of the African philosopher John Mbiti that, for the African, traditional religions permeate all the departments of life, so there is no distinction between the sacred and secular, the spiritual and the material. Also, to be human is to belong to the whole community. 'A person cannot detach himself from the religion of his group for to do so is to be severed from his roots.'

By meeting that deep ancestral need for a sense of community and by providing immediate and continuing contact with Jah the Rastafarian movement has become a major cultural force.

Another major creative force – though at first sight it seems so unlikely – is the combination of government, private sector and voluntary organisations that support the effort to use culture to build a sense of nationhood. 'Jamaica strove to give form and purpose to the idea of its people's creative energies and cultural achievements informing nation-building and the shaping of a new society.' There is no regimentation. Each artist freely portrays in wood and on canvas, in stone and in music, in dance, song, prose, poetry his emotions and thoughts, while the nation, through a variety of institutions and policies, provides training, public festivals and performances, private enterprise runs galleries, promotes shows and international events, and produces books and recordings. 'On one level is a fascinating story of a judicious mix of individualist vision and officialdom's enthusiasm and commitment.' (Nettleford.)

Bob Marley's statue *opposite*
[JAMAICA TOURIST BOARD, KINGSTON]

Nelson Cooper's 'Face of Jesus'
(pastel on paper) [ANDREAS OBERLI]

An example of this 'mix' is the Institute of Jamaica, organised in 1872 by a colonial governor to promote art, science and literature, and now charged to carry out its mission in the greatly enlarged setting of independence. It functions through a National Library which includes the famous West Indian Reference Library; a National Gallery which under expert direction, has become a show case of Jamaica's cultural growth; a Cultural Training Centre which includes Schools of Art, Dance, Drama and Music (teaching and research), a National History Division, an African-Caribbean Institute, a Museums Division and a Publications Division which publishes the well-known *Jamaica Journal*. A visitor, by contacting any of these agencies or such Government Agencies as the National Heritage Trust, can obtain information about policy and programmes.

Painters and sculptors

A recently published work, *Jamaican Art, an overview with a focus on fifty artists* is recommended. It tells how the Jamaican Art Movement began with a gifted group of pioneers in the 1930s, identifies the major influences that shaped their painting and sculpture, describes the growth of the movement and points to the new directions that artists are taking.

The book is beautifully illustrated. It is the first work of its kind and it reveals the extraordinary richness and variety that are the strength of Jamaican art.

The book is more than a history of art in the narrow sense. It takes us into the world of the Jamaican artist, brings us face to face with the dynamics of the Jamaican life-style, and it portrays the work of 'self-taught artists – Africa incarnated', the Ras Tafarians in particular.

Poets, actors, and 'Sistren'

Neither the painters nor the sculptors have the stage to themselves. The dramatists have transformed Kingston into the most active West Indian centre for theatre in much the same way as the musicians have made it the capital of a flourishing and profitable production enterprise, while a group of women poets have widened and deepened the range of West Indian literature.

The story of 'Sistren' reveals the involvement of people at the grass-roots in the cultural movement, and provides yet another example of the power of the indigenous as a dynamic force.

Sistren Theatre [SISTREN COLLECTIVE]

Lionheart Gal gives the life-stories of twelve of the 'Sistren' (Sisters) who belong to the group. All but two of the stories are in dialect. They tell, frankly and graphically, what life is like for a very large number of Jamaican women – and they reveal also the strength and courage of the folk, the depositories of so much of the spiritual power of a people.

Sistren describes itself as an:

> *independent women's cultural organisation which works at advancing the awareness of its audiences on questions affecting Caribbean women ... It is a collective which developed from the initiative of working-class women in 1977 and is best known for its popular theatre work. Its many plays deal with issues such as women's work, sexuality and women's history. Its dramatic problem-solving workshops derive from research with women and involve the audiences to analyse their collective situation and to seek solutions to pressing issues ... The Group's cultural work is rich in imagery derived from the music, dance and popular expression of the Caribbean.*

National Dance Theatre Company *opposite*
[JAMAICA TOURIST BOARD, NEW YORK]

Add the poets by turning to an excellent collection of Jamaican poetry since Independence, *From our Yard*, edited by Pamela Mordecai. Yet again we note the range and diversity of the work, and the extent to which the poets also are preoccupied with some aspects of the real lives of ordinary people. In the editor's words:

Whether it does or does not explicitly encourage people to be patriotic and proud of their heritage, pride in the racial, cultural and historical circumstances that contribute whatever we mean when we say 'Jamaica' is increasingly evident both in what these poems talk about and the language in which they talk about it.

The collection is a guide to the works of individual poets which are obtainable in local book stores. Among them is Lorna Goodison, whose poetry, as Pamela Mordecai points out, is typical of almost the whole body of poetry in the collection, in 'the Father requiring us to look to the condition of [our] part of this yard, this world which we share with the rest of mankind'. Jamaican poetry 'has grown into a sober valuing, not just of the beauty of the country but of every aspect of the lives of the people who occupy this part of this yard'.

Part of a Carnival procession [JAMAICA TOURIST BOARD, NEW YORK]

Music and dance

Music and dance are everywhere: in festivals, Carnival, in the National Dance Company's performances (the Company is now in its 30th year), in the annual Sunsplash memorial to Bob Marley, in the Negril Carnival and countless performances throughout the year.

The definitive work on the dance is Prof. Rex Nettleford's *Dance*, a large, richly illustrated volume which documents in narrative and in photographs the 30-year-old effort of the Jamaica Dance Theatre Company to carry out its mission of creating dance forms that faithfully reflect the realities of our Caribbean life and being.

Athletics, sports and world standards

Athletics and sports have an honoured place in Jamaican culture, and Jamaica's athletes and sportsmen have both brought honour to their country and dramatised the difference between size and quality. Spend a moment or two in the company of two of the country's great runners and its greatest boxer.

Today Merlene Ottey is one of the great female short sprinters

Polo players at sunset
[JAMAICA TOURIST BOARD, KINGSTON]

Windsurfing [JAMAICA TOURIST BOARD, KINGSTON]

Golfing [JAMAICA TOURIST BOARD, NEW YORK]

Hot air Balloon Festival (Roy O'Brien)
[JAMAICA TOURIST BOARD, KINGSTON]

Playing polo [JAMAICA TOURIST BOARD, NEW YORK]

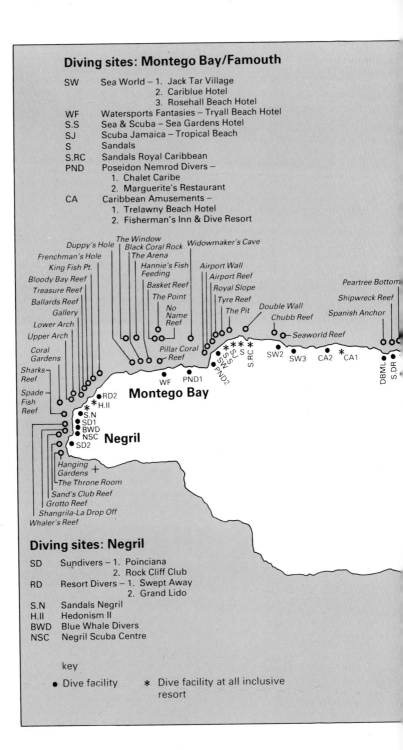

Diving sites: Montego Bay/Famouth

SW	Sea World – 1. Jack Tar Village
	2. Cariblue Hotel
	3. Rosehall Beach Hotel
WF	Watersports Fantasies – Tryall Beach Hotel
S.S	Sea & Scuba – Sea Gardens Hotel
SJ	Scuba Jamaica – Tropical Beach
S	Sandals
S.RC	Sandals Royal Caribbean
PND	Poseidon Nemrod Divers –
	1. Chalet Caribe
	2. Marguerite's Restaurant
CA	Caribbean Amusements –
	1. Trelawny Beach Hotel
	2. Fisherman's Inn & Dive Resort

Duppy's Hole
The Window
Black Coral Rock
Widowmaker's Cave
Frenchman's Hole
The Arena
King Fish Pt.
Hannie's Fish Feeding
Airport Wall
Bloody Bay Reef
Airport Reef
Treasure Reef
Basket Reef
Royal Slope
Peartree Bottom
Ballards Reef
The Point
Tyre Reef
Shipwreck Reef
Gallery
No Name Reef
The Pit
Double Wall
Spanish Anchor
Lower Arch
Chubb Reef
Upper Arch
Seaworld Reef
Coral Gardens
Pillar Coral Reef
SW2 SW3   CA2   CA1
Sharks Reef
Spade Fish Reef
RD2
Montego Bay
WF   PND1
S.N
H.II
SD1
BWD
NSC **Negril**
SD2
Hanging Gardens
The Throne Room
Sand's Club Reef
Grotto Reef
Shangrila-La Drop Off
Whaler's Reef

Diving sites: Negril

SD	Sundivers – 1. Poinciana
	2. Rock Cliff Club
RD	Resort Divers – 1. Swept Away
	2. Grand Lido
S.N	Sandals Negril
H.II	Hedonism II
BWD	Blue Whale Divers
NSC	Negril Scuba Centre

key

● Dive facility   * Dive facility at all inclusive resort

Diving sites: Ocho Rios/Runaway Bay

FD   Fantasea Divers – 1.   Sans Souci
                                    2.   Boscobel
OW   Oras Watersports – Silver Seas Hotel
G   Garfield's Diving Station – Mallard's Beach
WE   Watersports Enterprises – 1. Divi Beach Resort
                                          2. Mallards Beach
S.D.   Sea & Dive Jamaica – 1. Couples
                                2. Shaw Park
RD   Resort Divers – I. Jamaica Jamaica
                              2. Franklyn D. Resort
S.DR   Sandals Dunn's River
S.OR   Sandals Ocho Rios
J   Jamaqua – Club Caribbean
SD   Sundivers – Ambiance
DBML   Discovery Bay Marine Laboratory

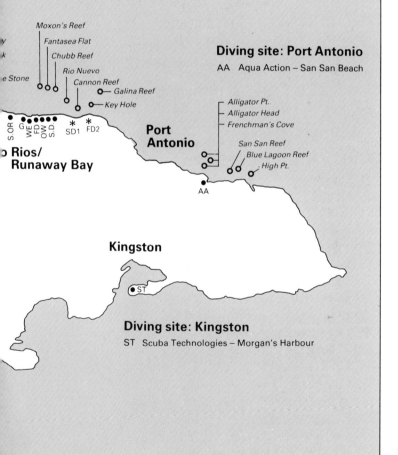

Diving site: Port Antonio

AA   Aqua Action – San San Beach

Map labels:
Moxon's Reef
Fantasea Flat
Chubb Reef
Rio Nuevo
Cannon Reef
Galina Reef
Key Hole
e Stone
S.OR
G
WE
FD
OW
S.D
SD1
FD2
Port Antonio
Rios/ Runaway Bay
Alligator Pt.
Alligator Head
Frenchman's Cove
San San Reef
Blue Lagoon Reef
High Pt.
AA
Kingston
ST

Diving site: Kingston

ST   Scuba Technologies – Morgan's Harbour

in the world. Brought up in a Jamaican country parish, her career as a runner began when she won a bronze medal at the 1979 Pan American Games in Puerto Rico. A year later she won the bronze medal in the Moscow Olympics, then, in 1989 she won the 200 metres at the Second World Indoor Championships. Since then she has held her place as one of the outstanding women runners of our time.

Donald Quarrie, another Jamaican runner, is one of the greatest short sprinters of all time. He has represented Jamaica in five Olympic Games, won the gold medal in 1976 at the Montreal Olympics, and taken medals in his fourth and fifth games. Few runners can equal his record.

Boxing

In 1984 Mike McCallum defeated Sean McMannion and took the world junior middle-weight title from his opponent. Just two years later three Jamaicans were holding three world titles, all at the same time: Trevor Berbick, Lloyd Honegan and Mike McCallum. Nettleford points out that, though we cannot in fairness claim Honegan as our own, he identifies in dress and musical tastes with his roots, 'his theme song being the reggae hit "Ragamuffin" and when he repeats . . . that "he tykes no prisoners" and is not "paid to fight overtime" it may be a cockney accent carrying the words but it is also authentic channelled Jamaican aggression'. McCallum himself, on the strength of the length of time (four years) he held the junior middle-weight title, and his six title defence victories, is one of the dominant sporting figures of the 1980s.

Cricket, football, cycling and other major sports regretfully do not appear in what is admittedly no more than a sampler of Jamaica's record in sport. The record is good, and in the case of cricket spectacular. Each has its national association and welcomes enquiries.

Entertainments and activities

The Jamaica Tourist Board publishes each year a calendar of cultural and sporting events. It is comprehensive, covering national festivals, international tennis tournaments, international marlin deep-sea fishing tournaments at Port Antonio, Montego Bay and Ocho Rios, international festivals such as the famous Sunsplash and Bob Marley festivals.

Water sports and diving

The sea is a constant companion offering swimming, water-sports, spectacular reef-gardens, scuba diving and deep-sea fishing.

Hotels by the sea have facilities for watersports. The centres that specialise in scuba-diving are shown on the map.

Reefs are easily destroyed and Jamaica appeals to all its visitors to help in preserving its priceless off-short reefs fashioned through millions of years by volcanic action and coral insects. An enthusiastic skin-diver, Dolores Keator, described them.

This glorious island is surrounded by an equally glorious undersea world: breath-taking valleys with pie-crust coral trees and staghorn corals so very like the antlers of deer, treacherous cliff faces with great crags and sheer drops into canyons that glow with the colours of amethyst, topaz and burnt sienna.

The University of the West Indies has a research laboratory at Discovery Bay, which specialises in the study of coral reefs. Situated close to one of the world's most interesting buttress reefs, it attracts marine biologists and divers from many lands.

Annual marlin fishing tournaments draw large numbers of fishermen to Port Antonio, Ocho Rios, Montego Bay and Black River, but devotees of deep-sea fishing will find abundant opportunity throughout the year for indulging in their sport at north coast resorts, Negril, and at such south coast resorts as Treasure Beach and Bluefields.

Diving on the reefs *overleaf* [THEO SMIT, POSEIDON NIMROD DIVERS]

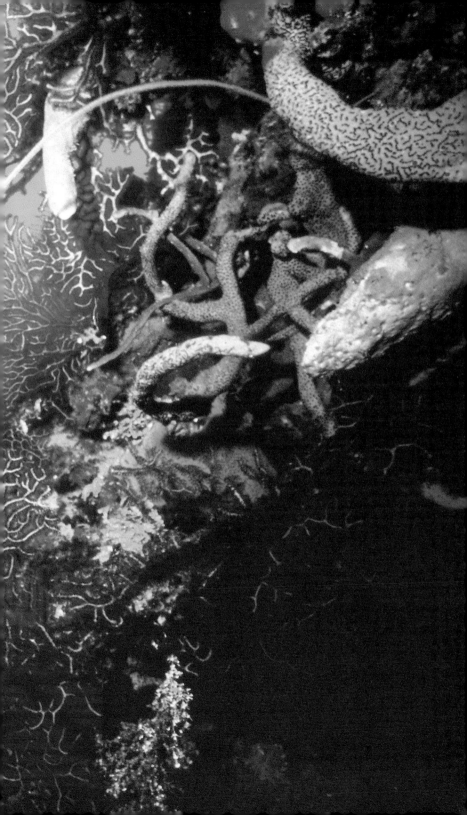

| 6 |
The folk and the cuisine of Jamaica

Jamaicans make poetry in the kitchen. The tradition of flavourful cooking was established by generations of women who started from girlhood and, as grannies, performed miracles on a raised fire-place, with one or two iron pots black from use, one or two bowls of clay called yabbas, and sticks of firewood. There were always one or two in a village who 'cooked sweet', earning the envy of other women and the respect of all the men with their fricasseed chicken, ackee and salt-fish, dip-and-fall-back, rice and peas, and scaveeched fish. They had no clock, no timer but the sun and an inbuilt sensing-device that told them when the stew was ready, or when the wood-fire should be damped down. They had no books of recipes, just their memories, well-developed taste buds and skill in stretching scraps of meat and fish.

These women, whether they worked in the kitchens of the Great House, where meat was plentiful, or as cooks with the growing number of upper and middle class Jamaican families, or in their own kitchens, created the typical dishes of Jamaica. Climate and a new environment set limits. Fresh meat and fish had to be used quickly, or salted and cured. Salted cod, mackerel and pickled herring kept better and went further. Pigs, goats and chicken supplied most of the meat that was used, beef being more expensive and not so plentiful. 'Breadkind', the general name for starchy food, was varied, with different kinds of yams (not sweet potatoes, as in parts of the United States), sweet potatoes, bananas, plantains, cassava, eddoes and cocos, along with cornmeal and flour. There was a wide range of vegetables, such as calalu (a Jamaican form of spinach), pumpkin (for soups and as a vegetable but never for pies), cabbages, okra, tomatoes and the like, red kidney beans, locally called red peas, and gungo peas. Here are some typical dishes. There are many books dedicated to the excellence of Jamaican cooking.

Famous Jamaica dishes

Soups

The basic theory is that soup must have substance. This means thick soups rather than clear; not cream soups but soups thickened with vegetables and 'breadkind', and flavoured with thyme, marjoram and pepper. There are Jamaican versions of such favourites as oxtail soup, fish broth, coco soup, beef soup, and a 'cook-up', a meal in itself that will make a man 'strong as a cow', based on meat, chicken, salt pork and yams and cocos, like the sancocho of Latin America. There are several Jamaican soups that are particularly famous. The first is Jamaica Pepperpot, a glorious combination of calalu (spinach) chopped fine, okra, soup meat, pigs' tail, onion, garlic and coconut milk with a few shrimps thrown in for good measure. Scotch Bonnet pepper is commonly found in Jamaica. The pepper is cooked unbroken in the soup so that it adds flavour without heat. Broken, it is lethal. Then there is Red Peas soup, made from the most popular of all the family of peas and beans, the red kidney bean. In Latin America the equivalent is Black Bean soup. Ingredients for this soup should include soup meat and pigs' tail, coco, eddo or yellow yam, escallion, thyme and the unbroken country pepper. Basically the same ingredients are used for Pumpkin soup, which should be made from firm-textured pumpkin of a rich yellow colour. These are soups that lift up a man's soul and make him prophesy.

Seafood

The most highly-prized delicacies are lobster, crab, snapper and king fish. The lobster is in fact a large crayfish, tender and delicate in flavour. Much rarer nowadays is the black or mountain crab which lives in holes on the land and which in March or April goes down to the sea to lay its eggs. Picking crabs is a tedious business. The meat is flaked, seasoned, mixed with a small quantity of fresh bread crumbs, put back in the shell and baked. No one can bake enough.

Scaveeched fish (pronounced scoveitch) is much the same as the *escabeche* of Latin America. In Jamaica the fish is fried first, then

Sampling Jamaican wayside hospitality *overleaf*
[JAMAICA TOURIST BOARD, NEW YORK]

smothered with onion and vinegar and highly spiced with Scotch Bonnet pepper. Very popular also is fried fish. Scaveeched fish and fried fish are eaten with bammies, flat cakes made from cassava flour or meal, half an inch or more in thickness. They are baked or fried and thickly buttered.

Salt-fish, the salted cod from North Atlantic waters, the *bacalao* of Spain and Latin America, is cooked in many ways: as a stew with cho-cho and tomatoes or mixed in with rice, or cooked in with sweet potatoes. Easy to make and very popular are salt-fish fritters, made small in size and very crisp as hors d'oeuvres, or large, with a mixture of flour, for breakfast or lunch. A heavy version of these is stamp-and-go, so named because travellers would stop to buy these fritters at a wayside shop, with a piece of bread, then stamp-and-go. Other fun names are 'poor man fritters' and 'macadam', because they are tough as the asphalted road, and 'John stagger back', from the shock of attempting to bite through them.

The great dish is ackee and salt-fish. Jamaicans argue that a beneficent providence guides us; if it were not so how could the ackee travel from its home in West Africa to meet in Jamaica the salted cod of Newfoundland? Such a marriage must have been made in heaven.

Meat and poultry

The notable dishes are roast pork – the quality of Jamaican pork is excellent – curried goat and fricasseed chicken. East Indians, who came to Jamaica in the second half of the last century, brought with them their skill in making curry. Jamaican cooks soon became expert at it. Curried goat is a highly spiced peppery dish, but it can be made less inflammable without loss of flavour. The secret of fricasseed chicken is that it should be seasoned with onion, scallion and black pepper overnight. On the following day the pieces of chicken should be wiped dry and browned. Finally, a small quantity of water is added along with tomatoes and a pinch of ginger powder, and then the dish is simmered.

'Breadkind'

Any starchy food is 'breadkind'; ripe plantains can be included. Yam is the great staple. There are many kinds: yellow yam, Lucea yam, sweet yam, renta, St Vincent and yampie. They can all be boiled, or boiled and creamed, or baked in the skin, or crushed and baked with cheese sprinkled on top. In the Jamaican kitchen every visitor should play Columbus, and few discoveries are more delectable than a yampie or sweet yam, fine in texture, baked in the skin, buttered and served steaming hot. Other great favourites are candied sweet potato, baked or roasted breadfruit, green banana boiled and creamed, and fried ripe plantain.

Rice takes its place alongside yam as a favourite, and one of the dishes that all Jamaicans overseas dream of is rice-and-peas, sometimes called Jamaica Coat of Arms. In the Eastern Caribbean this is called peas and rice. The peas used there are pigeon peas, called congo peas; in Jamaica they are called gungu peas. In Latin America the peas are stewed and the rice cooked separately. Jamaica cooks the red kidney bean and rice together. Authentic rice-and-peas requires, first, thick creamy milk from a dry coconut (see page 74), cooked with 1 cup of red kidney beans made tender by soaking, and with rice, about three times the quantity of the peas, with some escallion, thyme and black pepper. A very small piece of salt pork is added after the peas have been boiled.

Desserts

If oranges and star-apples are in season, then the natural choice is matrimony, a memorable intermingling of orange juice with the edible pulp of the star-apple, a dash of evaporated or sweetened condensed milk, a pinch of nutmeg and some ice. In season for the larger part of the year are guavas, stewed when ripe and served with coconut cream. Baked ripe bananas, also served with coconut cream or heated in a skillet in a mixture of brown sugar and butter, then flambéed with rum, are delicious. Ice cream is often made from the juice of the sour-sop, which has a pleasantly fresh, tart taste of strawberries and apricots. Cold potato pone is served with coconut cream; banana fritters with a dash of fresh lemon juice. To start or finish a meal, an extraordinary assortment of fresh fruit is available.

In praise of bammies, patties and spinners

A **bammy** is a flat cake, made from cassava flour or meal. It is round, and from half to one inch thick. Originally this was the cassava bread of the Arawaks and of other mainland Amerindian people. The Africans who were brought to Jamaica learned from the Arawaks how to make 'cassava bread', and they gave to it a name that is not found elsewhere: 'bammy'. In the course of time an indigenous gourmet produced a 'cassava wafer' which can now be purchased in supermarkets.

At first glance a bammy looks, and feels, hard and dry. Soak it for half an hour in milk, then put it in a frying pan with a dab of butter and pan fry it over moderate heat until it is brown on each side. It can also be baked. Ten minutes or thereabouts will suffice, depending on the thickness of the bammy. It is a delicious accompaniment to cold meats, soups and stews.

The cassava wafers are more fragile, but no less delicious. Butter the rough side, heat them briefly in an oven or frying pan until golden brown, and serve them at breakfast, or with hors d'oeuvres – or at any time.

PATTIES deserve capital letters. They rate above United States' hamburgers, English pasties, fish and chips, or Latin American *tortillas*. They have a highly-spiced, well-seasoned filling of beef. This is wrapped in a tender yet crisp crust. Jamaicans travel with suitcases and packages of patties; today it is possible to buy patties in Miami, London, Toronto, New York and other cities to which Jamaicans have migrated. They should be eaten hot; altogether they are a satisfying, protein-packed meal.

Spinners are small dumplings, rolled in the hand, about an inch and a half long, not more than half an inch thick at the middle, and tapering at both ends. They are lighter than a full-blooded Jamaica dumpling, which can pull teeth, chewable, firm without being over-demanding, and are an essential ingredient in Jamaican soups. They are perhaps a little like the Italian *gnocchi* but have more substance.

Drinks for every conscience

Drinks are available for every palate and for every conscience. Coconut water is in great demand, especially cool and refreshing

Young Jamaica *opposite* [JAMAICA TOURIST BOARD, KINGSTON]

from a green nut, which the seller will open with a quick slash of his machete. If you would like to try the jelly he will split the nut open and slice off a tiny portion of the green outside for use as a spoon. Coconut water is good for one; it flushes out the kidneys, and is a valuable source of iron; with a dash of lime juice, it helps to lower the blood pressure. Many Jamaicans find it excellent with a dry light rum. Visitors soon learn that the coconut water from the green nuts is not the same as coconut milk, which is obtained from the dry nut by grating the flesh, adding some water and squeezing out the milk.

There are as many varieties of fruit juices and nectars as there are varieties of fruit. Some of the more exotic are the nectars made from guava (an excellent source of vitamin C), mango, sour-sop, paw paw (papaya), tamarind and granadilla. Is there anything more welcome at mid-morning than an ice-cold glass of freshly-squeezed juice from a navel orange?

For rum punch the most commonly used recipe is: One of sour (one part of fresh lime juice); two of sweet (two parts of honey or sugar); three of strong (the rum), and four of weak (water and ice). If it is convenient, frost the glass ahead of time, then mix, shake and take. A drop or two of angostura adds to the flavour.

The local beer, Red Stripe, is excellent, so much so that over the years it has built up a market in Britain, Canada and the United States.

Wayside eating places

Along the coast there are wayside stalls that sell fried fish, with bammy or hard-dough bread. The fish, usually sprat or snapper, is fried with red pepper, escallion, onions and vinegar. With the bammy or bread it makes an excellent meal. If by chance the fish is too peppery, the cook may be willing to prepare a milder version; but first try what has been prepared.

Roasted fish may also be available. The fish will probably be turbot or wenchman (from Welchman), or doctor-fish, so-called because it has a sharp movable spine like a doctor's lancet on each side of its tail. Herbs, spices and butter are put inside and around the cleaned fish, which is then wrapped tightly in aluminium foil and put over an open fire. This is well worth stopping and waiting for.

Cooking jerk pork
[JAMAICA TOURIST BOARD, NEW YORK]

Jerk pork and jerk chicken are popular wayside dishes. The word 'jerk' goes back a long way. In his book *Jamaica Talk*, Cassidy says it is a Spanish word of Indian origin, and it means preparing pork in the manner of the Quichua Indians. The process was taken over by the Maroons, who hunted hogs. Portland is traditionally the parish associated with jerk pork, but it is now widely available. The meat is seasoned with pepper and spices, then grilled over a flat fireplace; the smoke from wood, often guava or pimento, adds to the flavour. If breadfruits are in season, slices of roast breadfruit are a good accompaniment.

There are some interesting drinks available at the stalls, in addition to coconut water or beer. The most popular is Sky Juice, or Earth Juice, a non-carbonated drink made from a syrup with a fruit base, mixed with crushed ice and water and served in a plastic bag with a straw.

Wayside eating places have multiplied in recent years. Here are some of the most popular.

Country near the docks in Port Royal. It sells fish soup, fried fish and bammy. These are also available at stands in the town. Port Royal is a centre for fishing, and the fried fish is good, as is the fish broth or soup, which is esteemed as an aphrodisiac.

Button Bay is just beyond Yallahs, on the road from Kingston to Morant Bay. This is a small fishing centre, so fresh fish is the attraction. Fish and fish soup are available at weekends. Hard-dough bread is the standard accompaniment.

Faith's Pen four miles east of Moneague on the main road (A3) to Kingston, is one of the gastronomic centres for those who travel by road. A dozen or more stalls offer roasted yam with a sliver of salt-fish roasted in the embers (and high in sodium, alas), boiled corn on the cob (a hard grained variety of yellow corn), ripe bananas and, in season, sweet-sops, sour-sops and avocado pears. Also on sale is soup, the most popular being cow-cod soup, which has been described as being full of bull, which means the procreative parts.

Ocho Rios has jerk pork and chicken and, in season, roasted breadfruit. There is a stall just west of the clock tower in the town. Some stalls can be found alongside the road to the Dunns River Falls, offering fried fish, jerk pork and jerk chicken. There are also stalls at the entrance to the Dunns River Falls. The meat is smoked over logs and branches from the pimento tree, which contain some of the spicy fragrance of the pimento berries.

Runaway Bay has a bar that sells fried fish by the pound.

Negril has its own way with the world and with the English language. A stall in the Plaza proclaims that it has for sale saucy perilla (sarsparilla), chainy root, Irish mash (Irish Moss), lynseed, blood whis, strong back, log wood honey and nutmeg, all served together in one drink. In the same plaza a family-run bakery sells excellent home-baked bread and pastry, as well as some Jamaican dishes, such as ackee and salt-fish baked in a stick of French bread.

Bluefields Beach has roadside stalls that sell fried fish, bammy, shrimps and river crayfish boiled with salt and hot pepper.

Middlequarters is a popular centre for crayfish and fresh water shrimps (which are often pronounced 'srimps' or 'swimps' and which are called 'janga').

From **Porus** to **Clarendon Park** the stalls are gay with fruit, golden oranges and tangerines, yellow grapefruit and ripe bananas, as well as with some ground provisions. In the season packets of freshly roasted cashew nuts are offered for sale.

Most of the wayside stalls offer bread of one kind or another; usually tightly-kneaded, chewy hard-dough bread. Jamaicans delight in bread. Every township in the island has its bakery, each with its own special way of mixing the dough and baking; with its unique way of shaping the loaves, its own special highly-glazed buns and flour-cakes or bullas. The standardised, artificially enriched bread of the world's great urban cities has no charm for a Jamaican. One of the most welcome gifts a Jamaican in exile can receive is an Easter bun or a loaf of hard-dough bread from home.

Cuisine and culture

The cuisine of a country mirrors its culture, its values, history and modes of expression. The Jamaican folk fashioned a cuisine of their own and developed a philosophy about food. Those who know hunger know also that 'Better belly bus' (burst) than good bitle (victual) spoil'. Those who know hardship learn how to share what little they have. They despise those who are mean or 'cubbitch' (covetous). To be greedy or 'craven' is contemptible. To be generous is to join the band of 'deastant' people.

| 7 |

Agriculture – a way of life

My own piece of rockstone

Agriculture affects all Jamaica. About twice as many persons are employed in agriculture as in the next largest sector, manufacturing, and five times as many as in the third largest, construction.

The numbers give some idea of quantity but in Jamaica agriculture

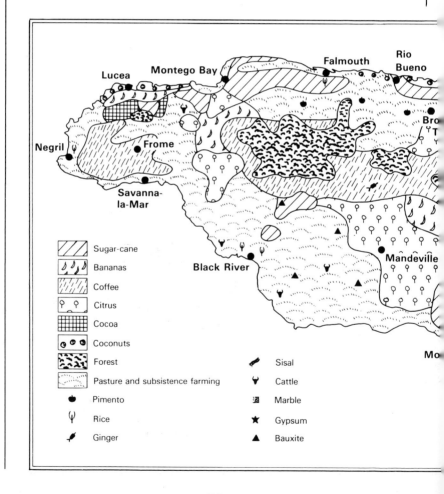

Sugar-cane	
Bananas	
Coffee	
Citrus	
Cocoa	
Coconuts	
Forest	
Pasture and subsistence farming	
Pimento	Sisal
Rice	Cattle
Ginger	Marble
	Gypsum
	Bauxite

has to do with dreams as well as with cash, with a man's self-image and role in society as well as with ploughing and hoeing, with emotions and values as well as with processing and marketing produce. It is both a system of production and a way of life.

Even in these times of urban sprawl the Jamaican dream is still, for many, land and a house. There is a steady movement of people and of produce from town to country and back again. Families remember how grandfather rented an acre of hillside land from the estate owner, planted it out and was evicted while the yams and sweet potatoes were still in the ground. If they cannot buy they will rent, but ownership means security and freedom from control. The distrust is there even when the Government is the landlord. 'They

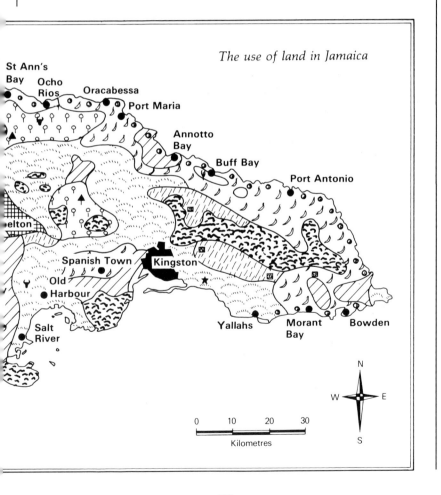

The use of land in Jamaica

won't sell it,' the peasant reasons, 'but they will rent it to we because they want to control we.' Every landless Jamaican dreams of the day when he will own what he affectionately calls 'his own little piece of rockstone'.

Land use and land distribution

Jamaica grows a variety of crops because of the differences in the elevation, temperature, climate and soils. The map shows how the land is used and where particular crops grow.

The plains and the mountains made possible the development of two systems of agriculture. One is based on large holdings of land which produce crops for export and some food for the home market, and the other is based on smallholdings, which provide some surplus for export and a large part of the local food supply.

History determined that the dual system should reflect the two societies which shared the island for nearly three centuries, one white and privileged, holding large tracts of land, the other black, exploited and without access to political power. Today independent Jamaica has established a national identity, and insists on equality of opportunity and freedom. The two systems of agriculture will continue, but now they mirror one society.

The estate system

The older system is that of plantation or estate agriculture, in which large holdings of land and a large labour force formed a unit for mass-producing one or two crops for export. The oldest sugar estate belt in Jamaica lies between Montego Bay and Falmouth. The story is written in the landscape, in the fields of sugar-cane that still flourish and in the ruins of old estates, such as the Running Gut Estate by the Rose Hall golf course. The Rose Hall Great House, Rose Hall Estate, Cinnamon Hill where the Barrett Family lived, and Cinnamon Hill Estate awaken echoes of the days when sugar was king.

Many Great Houses are in disrepair or in ruins. The planter families have disappeared. The production system based on free masters and black bondsmen was destroyed in 1834, the date of emancipation. A visit to any sugar estate within easy reach, however, will show that the basic patterns of cultivation and of production remain the same. Sugar-cane is a crop that is most efficiently cultivated in large units on flat or gently rolling land. Sugar is a manufactured product, in which the juice is extracted from the cane, boiled, converted to sugar and refined. The fields have to be within easy reach of the factory because the juice must be extracted within a day or two of the harvesting of the cane. Otherwise, the juice ferments and the crop is lost.

The smallholdings

The smallholding system came later. It grew out of the estate system, which was based on a large labour force of African people. This labour force had to be fed. The more the cane-fields spread, the more the demand for labour increased; the larger the labour force the greater the demand for food, for salted and pickled fish, flour and cornmeal from Boston and Savannah and Charleston, as well as for other plantation supplies. The estates allotted patches of 'hillside land' or 'mountain land' to the slaves for growing 'breadkind', yams, sweet potatoes and the like. When war interrupted the lifelines from North America, or when hurricanes destroyed the provision grounds, blacks died from starvation. More than fifteen thousand people were lost in this way between 1780 and 1787.

Immediately after emancipation many of the 'new frees' set off into the hills to found free villages of their own, and to lay out provision grounds, often with the help of Baptist and Methodist missionaries. In this way Jamaica gained its black peasantry, its system of smallholdings and some of its most important crops, among them the banana.

Bananas – and the smallholder

Banana cultivation contrasts sharply with that of sugar-cane. The banana tree is equally at home on a smallholding, a patch or a planta-tion. It is fast-growing, requires little care, calls neither for special equipment nor a factory. It has only to be ripened to be enjoyed as fruit. The banana is packed full of such essential minerals as potassium, calcium and iron, and is almost wholly alkaline. The peasant knows little of the nutritional details, but he knows that green and ripe bananas add greatly to his food supply and earn him a quick return on his labour.

Country market and trader women

Statistics and diagrams take on flesh and blood in country markets, and where better can a visitor see, pictured before him, the produce of the land and the way of life of rural Jamaica?

The hubbub begins on Friday afternoon. Buses packed to capacity with passengers and produce plough through the narrow streets,

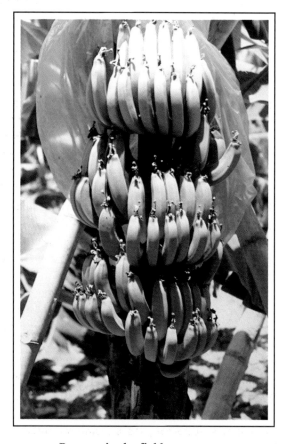

Bananas in the field [CAROLINE LEE]

scattering pedestrians as a strong breeze scatters leaves.

By Saturday morning the market is in full swing. A few of the traders are men: there are some butchers in white aprons at their stalls; two or three men with machetes standing by a truck laden with green water-coconuts; a man selling 'wet sugar' and jackass-rope, a long twist of tobacco leaves, half an inch in diameter, prepared for smoking and sold by the inch; a man with a brightly-painted hand cart with a large block of ice and bottles of thick sweet syrup, yellow, red, purple, green. This is a world dominated by women traders. Many of them are substantial in build and are also women of substance. Mrs Smith, presiding over a heap of yellow yams and sweet potatoes, has a daughter studying at university; Aunt Liz, with her scale and calalu, cucumbers, tomatoes and okra, has a son working in Toronto. They carry on their business with an easy air of authority, tough yet generous, bred to hardship, yet gentle. Their authority extends far beyond the market for, however assertive the men may be, the mother and grandmother are dominant in rural Jamaica, and the society of which they form a part is in many respects matriarchal.

The women traders have a long history of itinerant trading. Over the generations, on foot or astride a donkey, they established an internal marketing system which moved the goods from remote holdings, by hillside tracks and by dirt roads, to villages and towns. Trading is in their blood. They are intrepid entrepreneurs, undaunted by circumstances, eager to grasp at opportunities. From head-carrying, donkeys and hampers they moved to cars and buses and to markets beyond their parish; and now, as informal export-import traders, knowing little Spanish and less French, they travel by plane and bring Miami, Port au Prince and Panama into their trading system.

For buyer and seller trading is both business and a social occasion. Buying escallion and yams involves swapping news. Goods are for sale but gossip is free. There is a ritual for bargaining. Regular customers look at the goods they have bought and ask 'Where is my mek-up?' The seller laughs and hands over one or two red peppers or a tired tomato. If some vegetables are in short supply, what is scarce is married to what is plentiful; if 'sweet yam', for example, is scarce, it is 'married' to cassava, which is plentiful. Divorce is out of the question, for whom the higgler has joined together let no man put asunder.

Wayside stalls

The wayside stalls are irresistible. Even from a long way off they signal to us to stop. Golden oranges, tangerines of a deep yellow, scarlet ackees threaded on long sticks, large glossy-green avocado pears, papayas (paw-paw) that weigh four or five pounds, yams, sour-sops, whatever is in season – and the owner of each stall composes his own creation-poem out of what he has grown or bought. Nearby a three-year-old sucks an orange. An elder chews a piece of sugar-cane. Two or three hens cluck away in the shade of the nearby cottage. A goat heavy with kid pulls at the grass by the side of the road. A pig and its litter of five root at a clump of bananas. The stall is an extension of the household, tended by grown-ups and by youngsters, a source of ready cash in an economy based in part on subsistence farming.

Often the man or woman tending the stall is ready to talk about the things they grow and the high prices they pay for the fruit and vegetables they buy; and perhaps about the family: seven children, of whom two have grown up and gone away; one is in the police force in Kingston; the other five are still at home, and the two acres of land he owns cannot buy all the clothes and shoes they need. But he is better off than his neighbour Hezekiah Brown who rents the five acres he farms. Hezekiah has been paying rent for twelve years; some months he cannot pay more than the interest. It is better to own, even if it's only a piece of stony hillside. What helps him, he says, is that his wife raises some chickens and keeps a pig. And she is a good cook. When yams are in season they eat yam, and he keeps in reserve a few hills of St Vincent yam, because one planting lasts a long time. It spreads itself under the ground, so it is a help in time of need. That is why we call it 'Come-here-fe-help-we' yam. The price of shop-goods has gone up in the sky; high, high; even salt-fish, that was once poor man's food, it has gone high out of reach. It is rich man's food now. Salt-fish gone join up with satellite. And goat mutton gone up there too. A little meat at weekend perhaps, and for the other days, his wife makes some corn-pork stretch a long way.

Some well-established holdings are models of an efficient three-

A smallholder rides out on his donkey to harvest his pimentos *opposite*
[JAMAICA TOURIST BOARD, KINGSTON]

tier system of cultivation with tree-cover from breadfruit, ackee and avocado trees. The trees give shade to a small patch of coffee trees and protect the soil. The homes have three or four rooms, and are beautifully kept. But there are too many people on the land, and much of the land is marginal; so the young especially search desperately for a future, in the towns perhaps, or even overseas.

Jamaicans also welcome opportunities for seasonal employment in the United States and Canada. An outstanding example of these programmes is the recruitment of West Indians to cut sugar-cane in South Florida. This began in 1943, so the West Indian labour force is now an intrinsic feature of Florida's sugar industry.

Research studies indicate that West Indian workers send back millions of dollars to the sending islands and show that there are three direct beneficiaries of the programme; the participating worker, the worker's home island and the Florida sugar industry.

With limited landspace and most of the exits closed, Jamaicans find themselves in a difficult position. They have brought down their birth rate. In order to provide employment for an expanding population they seek access to more markets in North America and they press for more investment in Jamaica from overseas. They are also working to increase the flow of visitors into the island because they wish to attract more foreign exchange and because they value the friendship and understanding of people from other countries.

The government and agriculture

Ever since independence in 1962 the Jamaica Labour Party and the People's National Party have made agricultural reform and improvement priorities, and much has been done. The Government is committed to increasing the agricultural potential of Jamaica by a rural development programme, incentives for producing export crops, strengthening existing commodity organisations for such crops as citrus, coffee and bananas; overhauling the marketing system to get more efficient distribution; providing opportunities for ownership; developing new irrigation programmes; expanding production in the major crops and promoting other crops such as sorghum, maize, castor bean and other oil-seeds and flowers.

One of the most important of the Government-subsidised agencies is the Jamaica Agricultural Society, which acts as a farmers' forum, provides an excellent information service, runs a number of Farmers' Stores that sell seed and supplies, and organises agricultural shows and training courses.

There are island-wide Commodity Associations which supervise the cultivation and manage the marketing of the island's major export crops.

The Ministry of Agriculture and the various Associations of farmers have set about developing non-traditional exports and breaking into new markets. Ground crops, such as yams and sweet potatoes are on sale in Brixton and Birmingham, New York and Boston, Toronto and Montreal. Fish-farming is expanding, and holds out promise of becoming an important revenue earner. So does horticulture. Banana production has increased, as a result of improved cultivation and marketing. Coffee has expanded, partly because more land is under cultivation and partly because of the efforts of the Coffee Producers Association. There are active Commodity Associations for most of the crops, all striving to increase production and exports.

Those who wish further information will find these addresses useful:

Agricultural Development Corporation
11 North Street
Kingston.
(Tel: 922-3043)

Agricultural Information Service
Ministry of Agriculture
Hope Gardens,
Kingston 6
(Tel: 927-1731)

Jamaica Agricultural Society
Publicity and Information Service
67 Church Street
Kingston
(Tel: 922-0610)

Other resources

The University of the West Indies has a strong Faculty of Agriculture, which is active in research and teaching. It concentrates on studies closely related to the needs of the Commonwealth Caribbean. It is closely associated with the Caribbean Agricultural Research and Development Institute, CARDI, a regional organisation supported by fifteen Caribbean governments.

Some of the bauxite companies that operate in Jamaica have done valuable work in assisting smallholders, improving livestock management and improving marginal and poor land.

Useful addresses are:

University of the West Indies
Public Relations Officer
Mona
Kingston 7
(Tel: 927-8837)

CARDI
University of the West
Indies
Kingston 7
(Tel: 927-1231)

| 8 |
The economy – challenge and response

The money earners

Leaving out agriculture, which are the chief revenue-earners? And how well is Jamaica responding to the challenge to pay its own way?

The money earners are Mining, Construction, Manufacturing and Tourism. Let us look briefly at each of these, taking as our guide the Economic and Social Survey published annually by Jamaica's Planning Institute. Visitors who are interested in learning more about Jamaica's trade and industry and its potential for development are urged to obtain copies of the *Survey* from the National Planning Institute, 30 – 40 Barbados Avenue, Kingston 5, Tel: (809) 926-1480.

Following on this, we will look at Jamaica's record as an independent developing country.

Mining – bauxite and gypsum

In its 1989 review of the economy the Planning Institute of Jamaica reported that the year

> . . . *was marked by strong positive performances in the major productive sectors. The Mining Sector recorded the stronger growth, increasing by 38 per cent. Activities in the bauxite and alumina sub-sector accounted for the major part of the increase. For the year, total bauxite production was 9652.4 thousand tonnes, 32.9 per cent above that recorded in 1988. The increased level of activity . . . was facilitated by the reopening of Alpart in the first quarter of the year, increased facilities for the disposal of bauxite waste and the introduction of a new levy/tax regime more favourable to investors . . .*

> *The buoyancy of the bauxite-alumina sector impacted*

89

*positively on employment during 1989. Employment in the
sector increased from an average of 5,975 in 1988 to 6,400
in 1989.*

More than a century ago a Government geologist, Sawkins, reported
that bauxite was present in the red earth, but no one was interested.
Hans Oersted, a Danish chemist, had produced aluminium in 1825,
but not until 1886 had Charles Hall of the United States and Paul
Herault of France invented, quite independently of each other, an
inexpensive method of making aluminium. Even after commercial
production started, however, Sawkins's report was neglected.

By the 1930s world demand for aluminium had risen prodigiously
and a bauxite rush was on, but not in Jamaica. Not until 1942 did
Jamaicans discover that they were living on one of the world's
largest deposits of bauxite. Surveys made in the 1960s showed that
the deposits of commercial bauxite exceeded 600 million tonnes.

The discovery of bauxite ore in the 1940s was made by chance.
A Kingston merchant and weekend farmer, Sir Alfred Da Costa, was
puzzled by the poor yields he was getting from crops planted on
parts of his estate at Crescent Park in St Ann. Analysis showed that
the soil contained almost fifty per cent alumina. Thereupon he

Mining bauxite [JAMAICA TOURIST BOARD, KINGSTON]

started negotiations that took Jamaica into the ranks of bauxite-producing countries. Reynolds Jamaica Mines recorded Sir Alfred's discovery on a plaque by the side of the Moneague-Kingston main road, near the Crescent Park Great House, about four miles east of Moneague.

By 1950 three alumina companies were at work in Jamaica: Reynolds Jamaica Mines, the Kaiser Bauxite Company and Alumina Jamaica, at the time a wholly-owned subsidiary of the Alumina Company of Canada, Alcan. They bought up large areas of land in central Jamaica, so as to safeguard their supplies, and started mining operations. Since much of the land had been used for cattle-rearing, the Government required that it should be kept in production until it was needed for mining. It required also that the topsoil should be replaced where land had been mined and that a programme of land-rehabilitation should be undertaken.

There are three stages in the production of aluminium. First, the topsoil is stripped away and the ore loaded on to trucks and taken to a central place for dry storage. Next, the bauxite is reduced to a chalky-looking white powder, alumina. Finally, the alumina is smelted and made into aluminium. It takes about three hundred pounds of bauxite to produce one hundred pounds of alumina. This in turn yields fifty-four pounds of aluminium.

Alumina Jamaica (ALJAM) pioneered the industry by building two plants to process the bauxite into alumina in Jamaica, the Kirkvine Works near Kendal and the Ewarton Works on the Ewarton-Kingston road. The company transports the alumina to a deep-water harbour which it built near Old Harbour, Port Esquivel, named after the first Spanish governor of the island.

The other companies decided to ship the ore to the United States for processing. Reynolds Jamaica Mines built an overhead bucket-trolley line, six miles long, to carry the bauxite from the company's Belmont plant near Moneague to its storage building and the deep-water pier on the western side of the bay at Ocho Rios. A sign marks the place, but the rust-coloured layer of dust that covers the building and smothers the nearby vegetation identifies the place much more loudly. The Kaiser Bauxite Company built a terminal on the south coast at Port Kaiser, and another on the north coast at Discovery Bay and laid down a railway thirteen miles long from Tobolski near Brown's Town to its dry storage building beside the bay. This is linked to the pier by a conveyor which runs under the motorway, and which can load thirty-eight thousand tonnes on to a ship in ten hours. Ships approach the pier by a channel forty feet deep and four hundred feet wide, made by blasting away a part of the offshore reef.

The bauxite companies have made massive investments in Jamaica, and followed a liberal public-spirited policy. They knew that open-face mining leaves great scarlet gashes in green pastures, and that many Jamaicans were upset at the sight of monstrous bull-dozers tearing up the fields and at the thought of the earth of their country being carried off to foreign parts. But Jamaicans realised that the impact was not wholly one of extraction. They found satisfaction in the creation of deep-water harbours, roads and railways; in the replacing of the topsoil and the rehabilitation of the land; in afforestation; the rearing of beef-cattle; the provision of employment and a greatly increased flow of money. They valued the introduction of more sophisticated labour-relations than prevailed in the days when Jamaica's economy was wholly agricultural, and they found satisfaction in having modern technology in their country. They know, also, that Jamaicans hold positions of leadership in the industry, and that the companies respect and listen to the Government.

Visitors from large countries know how the economies of their own countries are hurt by a slow-down. They will understand how it hurts small countries that have few options.

Gypsum is mined in the mountains just east of Kingston harbour. There are plans for expanding this as a base for a viable gypsum board industry. In addition, deposits of marble, peat and clay are being investigated.

Manufacturing and construction

Jamaica is not in a position to choose between agriculture and industry. It has to improve and expand agricultural production for export and for greater self-sufficiency, and at the same time to expand agri-industry and light industry. It also has to find new markets and to expand existing ones.

One answer to being small was to get together with other countries. In the late 1960s Jamaica, in partnership with other countries of the Commonwealth Caribbean, established a Caribbean Development Bank and a Caribbean Free Trade Area (CARIFTA) which later became the Caribbean Economic Community (CARICOM). This provided member countries with a much larger market in the Caribbean. At the same time, Jamaica and the other newly-independent countries established embassies and trading missions in North America and Western Europe, set about expanding their markets and provided incentives to attract investments from overseas. Jamaica is currently promoting investment in such manufacturing areas as garments, textiles, electronics, furniture, footwear, alcoholic beverages, chemicals and plastics, food-processing, handicrafts and pharmaceuticals. Investments in manufacturing industries may qualify for development and tax incentives. Encouragement is provided for production geared towards export and labour-intensive methods.

Under Industrial Incentives legislation various types of manu-facturing enterprises qualify for tax holidays, the length of the period running from five to ten years. Those industries which are capital-intensive, the capital investment being no less than $9.5 million, may be granted a tax holiday for ten years.

Returning to our guide, the 1989 survey of the Planning Institute, the report on Construction states that:

> *The Construction Sector continued its strong positive growth, registering a real growth of 19.3 per cent . . . The level of growth attained during the review year represented the highest level of growth in that sector in over two decades. Construc-tion activities . . . were to a large extent attributable to the reconstruction activities which followed the September hurricane . . .*

In contrast, agriculture showed a decline which was also due in part to the hurricane.

Fortunately, Gilberts do not arrive each year, but the hurricane's impact on the Jamaican economy in 1988 underlines the vulner-ability of all Caribbean countries to the acts of God and of man, especially with reference to the oil crisis and to low prices for the chief export crops.

Manufacturing, in the colonial period, was a very small sector of the economy. Its record of growth since the 1950s is impressive. In 1989 'real growth of 7 per cent was recorded, but the figures give only a part of the picture'. To supplement this, visit the supermarkets or some of the many boutiques in the cities. Pay a visit also to plantations and sugar-factories: to Appleton to see how sugar and rum are made; to Prospect with its pimento trees; to Brimmer Hall to see how bananas and coconuts are cultivated; to any of the other plantations for which tours are advertised in the tourist resorts.

Every supermarket carries a variety of Jamaica rums, ranging from light to heavy, from white to amber to dark. All rums are aged and bottled under Government supervision, the average time in cask being five years. There is also a liqueur-type rum, produced by Wray & Nephew, which is fifteen years old. Visitors should approach with great caution the new white proof rum sold in bars, locally known as 'cow-neck' or as 'rude to parents'.

The best-known liqueurs include Tia Maria, Rumona and Pimento Dram, a special favourite at Christmas time and a pleasant remedy for stomach-ache. Look out also for a group of 'Old Jamaica' award-winning and attractively packaged liqueurs, such as wild orange and coffee, produced by Dr Ian Sangster.

The shelves are laden with fruit-juices, jellies, marmalades and nectars, including such exotics as mango, papaya and tamarind. The processed foods include some excellent local soups, pepperpot, pumpkin, red peas and pigeon peas. Sauces abound, many of them fiery, so a drop or two will suffice. Best known of all, and a gourmet's item, is the well-loved Picka-Peppa sauce, richer and superior in flavour to any Worcester sauce. Nearby are various brands of coffee, some specially packaged in air-tight tins for export. And, of course, there are cigars. Royal Jamaica won the 1969 and 1971 Brussels Gold Medal for making the finest handmade cigars in the world.

The boutiques and specialty shops carry garments designed and made in Jamaica, attractive fabrics, jewellery, cosmetics and perfumes. Designer clothing and jewellery are among the 'best buys' in Jamaica. One of the interesting perfumes is Khus-Khus, made from the fragrant roots of the khus-khus grass. For generations Jamaican housewives put little bundles of the root in their linen cupboards amongst their sheets and towels, in the way that French and English housewives use lavender.

Most of these enterprises are new. I recall going into a supermarket in Ocho Rios and talking with the shopkeeper, who pointed to jar after jar of preserves, bottle after bottle of sauces and to tins of fruit

Straw market stall *opposite* [JAMAICA TOURIST BOARD, KINGSTON]

94

juices, saying, 'See that label? Product of Jamaica. That's a good name, man. The country is advancing, coming up in the world'.

But the mood has changed. The owner of a boutique in one of the resort areas said, 'We worked hard, we built up a good business, but we have so little foreign exchange, our money has lost value, prices are high, and what kind of a future is there for the children?'

Many books about Jamaica and Jamaicans speak about an identity problem: that Jamaicans are people in search of an identity. Jamaicans know who they are. Their concern is not about identity but about security. The range of manufactured goods tells of the effort they have made. The faces show concern about the future.

The best furniture-making establishments are in Kingston and Montego Bay. The furniture industry, one of the oldest in the island, was established generations ago when owners of sugar estates brought out artisans and cabinet-makers from England to supervise the making of carts and mills for the estates and of fine furniture for the Great Houses. Beautifully carved four poster beds, of richly textured Jamaica mahogany, wardrobes, Windsor chairs and dining tables with elaborately-carved bases were the pride of the Great Houses. Some examples may be seen in Devon House in Kingston. Today Jamaican furniture finds a market in other Caribbean countries and in North America.

There has also been an extraordinary flowering of folk-crafts in straw-goods, carvings and sculpture, ornaments from shells and bamboo, and ceramics. Parts of the island are known for their fine work in straw. From parts of northern St Catherine come 'jippi-jappa' hats, beautifully woven from fine strips of palm-leaf in the style of Panama hats. The straw, and the hat, are named after the town of Jipijapa in Ecuador. Today handsome ladies' bags are made from this straw and from the coarser thatch palm, for which southern St Elizabeth is well known. In times past, straw hats were called trash hats, or thatch hats, or 'wha-fe-do' (what-to-do?) hats, a fun way of saying, 'This is the best I can afford'.

What is astonishing is the range of goods now being produced by the people. This is in part a result of pioneering work done by Jamaica Welfare, now the Social Development Commission; by some local organisations like MONEX and THINGS JAMAICAN; by pioneer entrepreneurs and by Government-supported training centres. Tourism has provided the stimulus of a market and of direct contact

Clay figurines [HERBIE GORDON]

between makers and buyers. The Kingston Crafts Market at the western end of Harbour Street, the Montego Bay Crafts Market, the Ocho Rios Craft Market with two hundred stalls for the display of work in straw, fabrics, wood and bamboo, and countless wayside stalls throughout the island bring visitor, producer and artist face to face. Questions about the work on display are welcome. Bargaining is part of the process of buying. Words of appreciation are valued.

Tourism

Jamaica is more than a resort and it has more to offer to interested visitors than sun and sea, fabulous though these are. The efforts now being made to diversify its attractions and to widen its range of offerings by tapping its secret attractions, such as the south coast, its spas, natural history, and the like, are beginning to show results. The Economic Survey reports that 'total visitor arrivals increased from 1 020 293 in 1988 to 1 163 236 in 1989. It was especially encouraging that the number of stop-over visitors increased by ten per cent while preliminary estimates of visitor expenditure showed an increase of about 12 per cent above 1987 and 1988.'

Challenge and response

There are notable achievements on the plus side. In the relatively short time since independence the nation has established a reputation for good government and for the orderly transfer of power from one political party to another by means of the ballot box. It has established most of the financial infrastructure that a modern developing democracy requires. It shares the general concern for human rights and the preservation of independence. It takes pride in the respect its diplomats have earned in the area of international policy. Its private sector is assuming a leadership role in nation-building. Government and private efforts have made primary education available to all its children.

But the major challenges of the independence period remain. The country depends on imported food and imported oil to meet more than 90 per cent of its needs for energy for its people, animals and machines. Ways have to be found of bringing idle lands and idle hands into production; of utilising to the full the natural creativity of the people; of creating a society in which income and ownership are more widely distributed.

These are difficult challenges for the most resourceful of nations where people are highly motivated to contribute to a national effort to build the economy. As Jamaica approaches the twenty-first century the national spirit must be galvanised to undertake these fundamental challenges and the strong spirit of individualism must be channelled into socially and economically productive activities. It is a delicate balance to be struck by delicate and sensitive national leadership. (Davies and Witter: *The Development of the Jamaican Economy since Independence*).

| 9 |
Montego Bay
and its surroundings

General information

The city of Montego Bay stands on a bay bearing the same name on the north-west coast of Jamaica, 18.28° latitude, 77.57° longitude. By air it is forty minutes from Kingston, by rail 113 miles and by the A1 north coast road 120 miles. There is little elbow-room for the city between the sea and a huddle of high hills behind.

With a population of 75 000, Montego Bay is second to Kingston in size (but, claim Montegonians, second in nothing else). It is the capital of the parish of St James (240 square miles) as well as the commercial and administrative capital of the county of Cornwall, which includes the parishes of Hanover (177 square miles) and Westmoreland (240 square miles). It has a deep water pier with berthing for four vessels, a free port area and the facilities of a modern city.

The Bay of Good Weather – Golfo de buen Tiempo – was the name Columbus gave to the bay when he discovered it on 9 May, 1494. Spanish settlers moved to the island in small numbers after 1510, settling first on the north coast around Seville, near St Ann's Bay. They brought with them cattle, horses and pigs, which were left to roam wild on the savannahs and multiplied prodigiously. In time sloops and schooners began to call at Montego Bay for supplies of lard and hides; goods much in demand in a Europe that depended on candles for its lighting and on leather jerkins and boots for its armies. The Spanish for 'lard' being 'manteca', the bay was called Manteca Bahia; less romantic, but easier to say, than the name Columbus gave it. Some of the English, who took the island from Spain in 1655, settled around Manteca Bahia and, in the prosaic mood of those who named Rum Cay and Magotty, they called it Lard Bay. By good fortune the Spanish form prevailed and it became Montego Bay.

Allowing for growth and for the changes wrought by modern

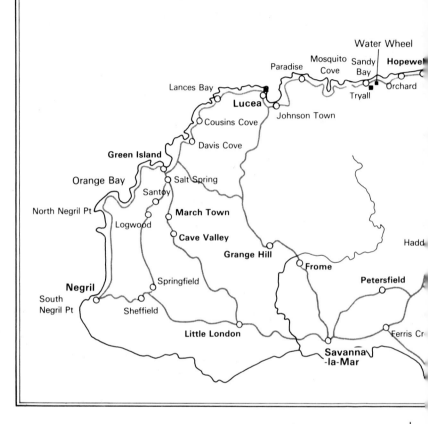

Montego Bay and the surrounding area

technology, the general impression of the city and its setting is much the same today as it was in 1802 when Maria Nugent, wife of the Governor of Jamaica, visited it.

> *The town of Montego Bay is situated in an amphitheatre of very high hills. In front a most beautiful bay, full of vessels and open to the sea. On the hills are all the gentlemen's houses, or those not immediately shopkeepers. These are interspersed with gardens, palms, etc of all sorts. So that from the town, quite up to the tops of the hills, you see nothing but villas peeping out from among the foliage ...*

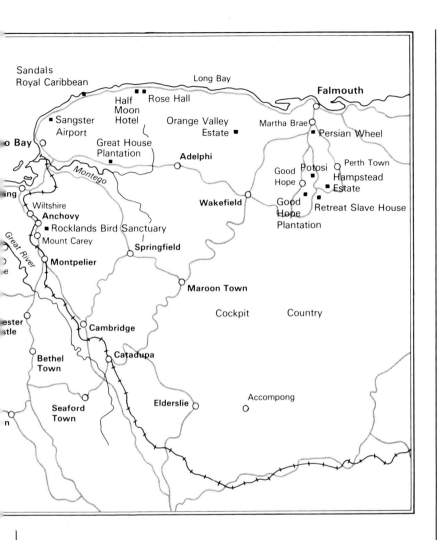

Sandals
Royal Caribbean

Long Bay

Falmouth

Half Moon Hotel   Rose Hall

Sangster Airport   Orange Valley Estate

Martha Brae

Persian Wheel

o Bay

Great House Plantation

Adelphi

Good Hope   Potosi   Perth Town

Hampstead Estate

ing

Montego

Wakefield

Good Hope Plantation   Retreat Slave House

Wiltshire
Anchovy

Rocklands Bird Sanctuary

Mount Carey   Springfield

Montpelier

Great River

ester
stle

Maroon Town

Cockpit   Country

Cambridge

Bethel Town   Catadupa

Seaford Town   Elderslie   Accompong

n

Reading the landscape, we find sugar-cane on the flat land to the east, in the direction of Falmouth and also to the immediate west of the city. To the west also, in the direction of Lucea, are bananas and coconuts. Behind, on the terraces and in the valleys of the escarpment, are bananas and citrus.

Buses and trucks hurtle along the coastal highways and the roads that lead down the escarpment, to unload passengers and produce at the city market and city centre. Visitors from cruise ships and hotels mingle with city dwellers on the streets, or loiter at wayside stalls. Montego Bay is market town, commercial centre and tourist resort and its colourful, agitated life signifies a natural blending of country and city, foreign and indigenous.

To this movement in space let us add another dimension, that of time. This dynamic intermingling grew out of relationships between North America and the island that began when both were young.

Some of the ships that Maria Nugent saw in Montego Bay Harbour were from the eastern ports of the United States: Wilmington, Savannah, Charleston, Boston, and probably also from Halifax in Canada. The island had molasses and rum, which the North American colonies needed, and which they used in part for their fur trade with the Indians. In exchange, the northern colonies provided the islands with flour, salted meat and cod, staves for puncheons, nails, candles, horses and other plantation supplies.

The North American trade routes to the Caribbean were vital arteries. When they were cut by war people in the islands died. Between 1773 and 1783 the slave population of Barbados fell from 68 000 to 57 400 largely as a result of famine caused by the interruption of the trade due to the American War of Independence. Jamaica also suffered great distress during the same period.

People and ideas moved, as well as goods. George Washington's brother spent a year in Barbados trying to regain his health. When Benjamin Franklin was establishing the Academy in Philadelphia he sent Dr Howell to the sugar islands to collect money. Alexander Hamilton, who knew a good thing when he saw it, was taken at an early age from Nevis to the United States. Between 1650 and 1790 there were at least eighteen West Indian and Bermudan students at such colleges as Harvard, William and Mary and King's College in New York. In 1720 a Jamaica-born Jew was lecturer in Hebrew at Harvard. In addition there were close family ties between scores of families in the United States and the West Indies.

It is worth looking more closely at one example of the many far-reaching results of this Caribbean-North American relationship, one that involved Montego Bay and profoundly affected Jamaica.

At the outbreak of the American War of Independence a number of loyalist families moved to Jamaica. Some were slave-owners. One was the master of George Lisle, who was permitted to preach, and who converted Moses Baker, the slave of another loyalist immigrant. Lisle set up a chapel in Kingston, and Baker and himself soon had more church members than they could serve. In search of help, they appealed to the Baptist Missionary Society in London and in response the Society sent out its first missionaries to Jamaica in 1814. Methodist missionaries soon followed.

In Montego Bay, at the corner of Market Street and King Street, is the Burchell Memorial Baptist Church, named after Thomas Burchell (1799 – 1846), one of these pioneer missionaries. Another pioneer missionary was William Knibb, whose name lives in the William Knibb Memorial Church in Falmouth, at the corner of George Street and King Street.

The preaching of the native Baptists, Lisle and Baker, and of the missionaries, was dynamite. They were bitterly opposed by the planters, who understood very well that to preach that all men are the sons of God was to set in motion dangerous ideas about freedom and equality.

The message lodged in the heart of a domestic slave, Samuel Sharp, who lived in Montego Bay and was one of the members of Thomas Burchell's church. Literate, intelligent and a powerful orator, he found an outlet for his gifts in a mission church and built up an independent connection with the native Baptists who looked at him as their ruler or 'Daddy'. His reading of the Bible, the news of the emancipation movement in England and the American declaration that men are created free and equal convinced him that the slaves should make a bid for freedom. He called for a non-violent bid in which lives would not be taken.

On Tuesday, 27 December, 1831, a fire on Kensington Estate in St James marked the beginning of a slave rebellion which swept the western parishes and which is called, in Jamaica, the Baptist War.

The slaves indulged in widespread destruction of property but there is no hint of a crusade against the whites. There were only two crimes of violence against white people throughout the rising. A Presbyterian parson testified 'Had masters, when they got the better hand, been as forbearing, as tender of their slaves' lives as their slaves had been of theirs, it would have been to their lasting honour . . .' They were not. They shot or killed two hundred and seven slaves and executed another three hundred and seventeen.

Daddy Sharp showed his genius by fastening on the one easily understood method: let every slave peacefully withdraw his labour. Gandhi and Martin Luther King were to employ this method of non-violence more than a century later. It is a measure of Sam Sharp's greatness that he fashioned this instrument against oppression. Sam Sharp was hanged. He told his friend, the Methodist missionary

Bleby, 'I rather die than be a slave.' He is one of the national heroes of independent Jamaica, and belongs to that great company of men and women of all nations and tongues who made freedom a part of our heritage.

The Cage that stands at the north-west corner of Charles Square, the old Courthouse on its west side, and the Brandon Hill Cave are reminders of the past and of Sam Sharp's affirmation of freedom. The Samuel Sharp Training College is his memorial. For Jamaicans, Montego Bay is more than a resort or commercial centre. It is one of the national shrines of Jamaica.

Now for the city

West Indian cities have had more than their share of fires and hurricanes; after these have come a deluge of developers who tear down the past to build the latest concrete cliché. Even so, places still survive where we can touch the past.

Charles Square, or the Parade, was laid out in honour of one of the island's Governors, Admiral Charles Knowles. The place, like the heart of the city, is tight-squeezed but there is a hint of graciousness.

The Old Court House stood on the west side of the square. For Jamaicans it is a place of shadows and pain. Here brutal George Gordon, captain of the local militia, presided over a court martial after the 1832 slave rising and sentenced hundreds to beatings and hanging.

At the north-west corner of the square there is a small building, The Cage, with a cupola, dated 1806, which was once used as a lock-up for runaway slaves, disorderly seamen and vagrants. Sunday was market day for the plantation slaves, when they came into town to sell their produce. At two p.m. the constable rang a bell to warn the country slaves to leave the city. He rang the bell again at three p.m. as a last warning. After that any slave found on the streets was put in 'The Cage'.

The Dome has more pleasant and romantic associations. Legend tells how a Spanish girl and her little slave companion were playing near the Dome, by a stream that supplied the town with water. They were hunting crabs out of their holes. The Spanish girl moved a stone under which a crab had scuttled and heard the sound of bubbling

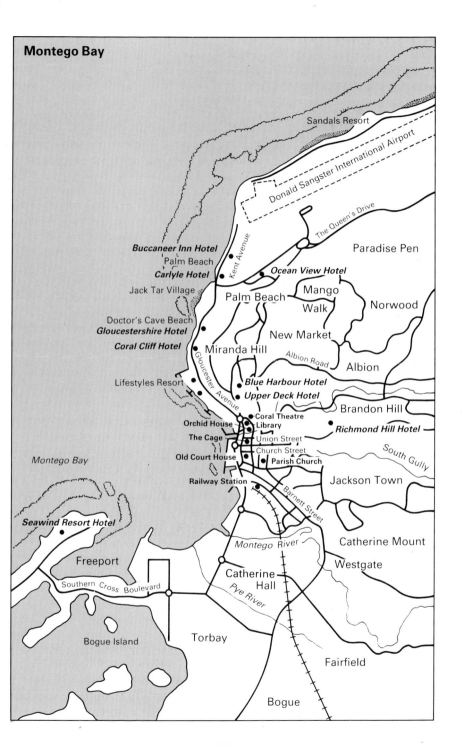

Montego Bay

water. So did the little slave. Frightened, they ran off to tell what they had heard. Half-believing, a few grown-ups went to the place, dug and found a spring. Delighted at finding this new source of fresh water, they freed the little slave and built the Dome to shelter the spring, which they called El Rio Camarones, Crab River. The present tower was built in 1837. The spring ceased being the town's source of water at the end of the last century.

Shopping is concentrated at the City Centre, where many of the in-bond shops are: Overton Plaza, the Holiday Village Shopping Centre where the Blue Mountains Gem Workshop invites visitors to see how the semi-precious stones are processed, and the Westgate Shopping Plaza. There are in-bond shops also at many hotels. Along Gloucester Avenue there are many booths with large assortments of Jamaican straw goods.

There are two places that should not be missed. One is the St James Parish Church, the city's great treasure. Cruciform, its foundations date back to 1778. In 1957 an earthquake destroyed the tower and so severely damaged the building that it had to be almost entirely rebuilt. This was done very skilfully, with very little change from the original. Pause for a minute or two to admire the limestone ashlar and the large round-headed windows that light up the interior so effectively, the mahogany fittings, the monuments which date back to the rich days of the plantocracy. The two most interesting are of Mrs Rosa Palmer, who should not be confused with the White Witch of Rose Hall, and Dr George McFarquhar. They are by John Bacon (1740 – 1799), the most celebrated English sculptor of his time, whose work also includes the Rodney monument in the square in Spanish Town.

The other is the market on Fustic Street. Europe touches Jamaica in the Parish Church, Africa in the market, with its 'enveloping sensory profusion and confusion'. Walking through these Jamaica markets, whether here or in Ocho Rios or Browns Town, it is possible to imagine oneself in the Yoruba and Ibo markets of Nigeria, which Wole Soyinka, Nigeria's great novelist, so vividly recreates; colourful markets, aroma-laden, markets such as one finds throughout West Africa, where sights and sounds blend together to form part of the country, the people, the past and the future, and to link together the three worlds that are for Africa one world, the ancestors, the unborn and the living. Here, instead of African fried bean cakes (akara) filled with green and red peppers and ground and

Cruise ship in Montego Bay Harbour
[JAMAICA TOURIST BOARD, KINGSTON]

chopped crayfish, there are fried fish, johnny cakes and bammies. The meats are different but the ritual is much the same, the reliving of a drama that was not cut short by a forcible transplanting from Africa to the Americas.

Excursions: Cornwall Beach

Cornwall Beach offers an underwater marine park; a long beach of white sand dotted with cabanas; water sports, scuba diving, snorkelling; a craft training centre where you can watch articles being made from straw and wood; a bar and cafeteria. On Saturday evenings there is a Jonkanoo Beach Party with masked dancers, limbo dancers, calypsos, dancing, and with goat and donkey races. The entrance fee covers the cost of a buffet supper and drinks at an open bar.

A harbour cruise

The CALICO cruises in the morning (10:00 a.m. to 3:00 p.m.) and afternoon (5:00 p.m. to 7:00 p.m.) offer an opportunity to see the city from the harbour, and to pick out some of the landmarks from the sea. The Freeport on the western side of the bay was made by reclaiming land and linking together a chain of mangrove-covered pancakes of land, known as the Bogue Islands. Call 952-9863 for information and reservations.

Evening on the Great River

This is fun, even though a mixture of natural charm and contrived amusement. The river setting is dramatic, for the trip is made at night in fishing boats manned by expert boat men, who take their passengers up a torch-lit river to an Arawak-style village. This has an open bar, dancing and a floor show.

Rocklands Bird Sanctuary near Anchovy

This excursion is recommended. The drive to Rocklands is an introduction to the natural beauty of rural Jamaica. The sanctuary is the life-work of a Jamaican, Lisa Salmon, internationally known as an ornithologist, who has created a sanctuary not only for birds but also for all people who find refreshment in nature, in birds, plants and gardens.

The sanctuary opens at half-past three in the afternoon. From then until dark is feeding time for the birds, and the porch of the house and the lawn are gay with the colour and movement of Jamaican humming birds, saffron finches, orange quits, the red-capped woodpecker and ground doves of soft slate gray. More than a hundred varieties of birds have been reported in the neighbourhood. Walks can be arranged for those who wish to explore further. Bird watchers or not, all visitors will find delight in the Forest Garden with its bird baths, ferns and shade plants of many kinds.

To get to Rocklands take the main road that leads from the city centre in the direction of Reading and Lucea.

At the junction to Reading, 4.8 miles west of Montego Bay, leave the coast road, turn left up Long Hill, on the road leading to Anchovy, and continue for 2.2 miles up the escarpment.

At the top of the hill look for the signpost for Rocklands on the left. You will come to Rocklands Bird Feeding Station half a mile further on, on the right.

Rose Hall Great House [OLIVER BENN]

Returning by the same route, you will enjoy the view of Montego Bay as you descend Long Hill.

One-day tours

The **Governor's coach tour** to Appleton is made by rail. Details should be checked with the Jamaica Tourist Board.

The other tours described here lie in the same general direction, east of Montego Bay, and are reached by the north coast highway, A1. It is therefore possible to combine some of the tours, for example, the tour of the Great Houses, with Falmouth and Oyster Bay; or the Great Houses and the Martha Brae. Good Hope and the Windsor Cave will take a full day. Possible combinations and the length of time should be checked with a tour operator or the Jamaica Tourist Board.

Great House tour

This tour can be combined with a visit to Falmouth and Oyster Bay and with rafting on the Martha Brae. Take the north coast road (A1) and travel east to the **Rose Hall Great House**, passing Ironshore Estate and the Rose Hall Golf Course. It is nine miles from Montego Bay. The House was built between 1770 and 1780 by John Palmer, at the time Custos of St James, at a cost of £30 000. It consisted of a rectangular building three storeys high with two wings of one storey each that enclosed a courtyard at the back. The interior was beautifully panelled in mahogany, cedar and rosewood. The north coast was open to attack by privateers in war-time, and John Palmer protected his new home with a small battery of guns, wisely so, for in January 1780 he was able to scare off a Yankee privateer, the 'Tartar of Boston, commanded by one Porter . . . she mounts 18 six-pounders on one deck, six smaller on the quarter deck and carries 118 men . . .'.

John Palmer lived beyond his means and had to mortgage Rose Hall a few years before his death. His grand-nephew John Rose Palmer inherited the property and lived there from 1820 to 1827, when he died.

The first mistress of the Great House was Rose Palmer who survived three husbands before marrying John Palmer. They lived happily together for twenty-three years. On her death John Palmer commissioned the famous sculptor Bacon to carve her profile on the monument in the St James Parish Church. This was the virtuous Mrs Palmer, whose manners were 'open, cheerful and agreeable', and who was 'warm in her attachment to her friends'.

In 1820 John Palmer's nephew, John Rose Palmer, brought his lovely young wife, Anne, to Rose Hall. Her beauty and wealth drew men to her, and her powers of witchcraft kept her terrified slaves submissive in spite of dreadful beatings and the agony of iron collars and spikes put on in her presence. After John's death in 1828 – who knows how? – she entrapped as lovers the book-keepers and overseers here and at Palmyra, and slaves as well, putting each to death when she tired of him. Whispers spread of bloodstains on the floor of an upstairs bedroom where a man died from a dagger wound and of an underground passage that led to the sea.

The story ran that

When mistress tire of the man she love
She make those two black slaves go throttle them
Den drag dem down dat passage to de sea
An' throw them to the sharks – dem tell no tales.

Her slaves hated her but dared not touch her because of her power as an obeah-woman. At last one of her lovers, finding he was falling out of favour, strangled her. None of her own slaves would bury the body. Planters brought their coachmen from near-by estates, buried her and marked the place with a square pile of masonry.

In the 1930s the celebrated medium Mrs Garrett visited Rose Hall. She became greatly disturbed at a spot in the courtyard which she identified as the resting place of Anne Palmer; and she reported that Mrs Palmer told her no one would ever find happiness at Rose Hall.

The story is told with embellishments by De Lisser in the *White Witch of Rose Hall*, and by Shore and Stewart in their book *In Old St James*. In recent years an historian, Geoffrey Yates, traced the second Mrs Palmer to a peaceful burial in the parish churchyard, but the Witch lives on in Jamaica's best-known horror story.

Cinnamon Hill Great House, a private property, abuts Rose Hall on the east. It belonged to the Barrett family, one of whose ancestors was a private in the English army which, under General Venables, took Jamaica from Spain in 1655. Elizabeth Barrett married the poet Robert Browning in 1846, against the wishes of her tyrannical father, Edward Moulton Barrett, who is portrayed in 'The Barretts of Wimpole Street'. Edward and Samuel had a sister, Sarah, the little girl in the famous painting 'Pinkie' by the great English portrait painter Thomas Lawrence. She died at the age of twelve. The painting is now in the Huntington Library in San Marino, California.

The Great House has been modernised, but it retains its 'cut wind', designed to break the force of hurricane winds, and hollowed out inside to form a vaulted shelter.

Greenwood House, fourteen miles from Montego Bay, dates back to the early 1800s, though with later modifications. It contains authentic furnishings and a valuable collection of eighteenth century musical instruments. The house is privately owned but its owners have opened it to the public.

Falmouth and the Martha Brae

Falmouth was once a busy sugar port, frequented by ships from Europe and North America, which called for the molasses and rum produced by eighty or more sugar estates. Traces of its past elegance remain in its Georgian buildings, Parish Church and the Palladian Court House with a double staircase.

Fires and hurricanes ravaged Falmouth from time to time, and a period of neglect set in after the decline of the plantation trade. But the town is rich in history. The William Knibb Memorial Church at the corner of Church and King Streets is named after William Knibb (1803 – 1845), son of a tailor of Kettering in the English county of Northamptonshire who came to Jamaica in 1825 as a missionary. After moving to Falmouth he earned the hostility of the planters because of his 'subversive' preaching to the slaves. During the slave rising of 1831 Knibb and other missionaries were arrested and sent to Montego Bay. Knibb made his way to England, gave evidence against the system of slavery before Parliamentary Committees, campaigned passionately for emancipation, returned to Falmouth in 1834, supervised the building of the Church (later destroyed by fire) and celebrated the granting of complete freedom with a midnight service at which the emblems of slavery, the chain, whip and iron collar, were buried. The scene is portrayed on a marble panel at the east end of the church, with Knibb's head at the base. It also has the profiles of the leaders of the English emancipation movement, Wilberforce, Sturge and Granville Sharp. In the churchyard are memorials celebrating the abolition of slavery.

Oyster Bay, 1½ miles east of Falmouth, gets its name from small oysters that cling to the roots of the mangrove trees. It has two inns, The Dive Hotel and Glistening Waters, a sea-food restaurant. The Bay is remarkable for its phosphorence which can be observed at night.

Martha Brae and Witchcraft A few houses 1¼ miles east of Falmouth, at the junction of a road to Duanvale, mark the site of the first capital of Trelawny, before the river silted up and Falmouth became the port.

Legend says the name Martha Brae is that of an old Arawak witch who knew of a gold mine by the river. Some Spaniards tried to find out the location from her. Martha Brae took them into a cavern full of human skeletons. Suddenly the river changed its course, poured through the cave, drowned the Spaniards and blocked the entrance for ever. Today the river is kinder to visitors, offering them off-the-beaten-track excursions. It also offers glimpses of the past through its Persian Wheel, which once lifted water from the river and poured it into a raised trough that supplied Falmouth.

The Martha Brae contains fish: mullet in the dam above the Persian Wheel, and tarpon and snook lower down, near the mouth of the river. The 'locals' can advise on the best times for trying one's luck.

More popular than fishing is rafting on the river. Excursions start at the Martha Brae rafting village, three miles inland, where there is a bar with restaurant. The cost of a rafting trip is US$30, but prices should be checked with the Tourist Board or with JADCO. Arrangements can be made through them.

Good Hope and Windsor Cave

There is something satisfying in a harmony of man's buildings with nature's work. Good Hope is an excellent example, and a visit is recommended.

Proceed from Martha Brae for 1.6 miles to a point where the road branches. Take the road to Good Hope, which is on the left-hand side. After one mile, at a junction, take the unpaved road. It leads through some of the old Trelawny sugar estates: Potosi with its derelict sugar works and Retreat Great House a mile further on, with a row of twenty-five low, one-roomed huts built of stone on the side of the hill. At a distance of 4¼ miles from Martha Brae you will come to Hampstead Estate; then drive through an avenue of bamboos beyond the entrance to Wales Estate, to arrive at last at Good Hope, 5½ miles from the starting point at Martha Brae.

John Tharp (1744 – 1804) bought the property – 3000 acres – in 1767. The owner of a Hanover estate, he married the co-heiress of Potosi. Together they bought up the neighbouring properties, to the point where it was said that Tharp could ride from the north to the south coast of Jamaica without leaving his own land. It is said that he owned 10 000 acres of land and 3000 slaves.

After John Tharp died, Good Hope fell on hard times. Sugar prices were low. The owners lived in England. The property was broken up and sold. It passed through the hands of people who had little interest in it. In 1912, a wealthy American banker, J F Thompson, bought it. He appreciated its historic value and its potential. His son, combining good taste with business acumen, turned Good Hope into a hotel. The property is now privately owned.

Look, first, at the buildings that make up the complex: the Great House, built about 1755, with a central block with high ceilings, and with wings on the left and right set at right angles, and a portico; a small two-storey counting house that is a gem; an ice house with a tablet recording when the estate was settled; and below the Great House the estate buildings, including a slave hospital, later used as an Anglican church, an estate office and a small building with a Palladian front that may have been used as a store. Having looked at all these, stand back and absorb the whole, including the sugar works on the bank of the river and the lovely old stone bridge. Buildings and landscape are in perfect harmony.

Look next at a superb example of the architecture of nature. Continue along the road to Wakefield and Sherwood Content and when the road branches, take the one on the left that leads to Windsor – not the one on the right that leads to the 'house in a hollow', or, in Welsh, Pantrepant.

You are now at the edge of the Cockpit Country. Drive for two miles through a narrow corridor of limestone to Windsor, now owned by the Kaiser Bauxite Company. After passing some Company houses you will come to a pleasant meadow ringed with vine-covered limestone cliffs. Old Windsor Great House stands in the centre. The path to Windsor Cave is about half a mile from the Great House to the right. Take the path that forks right, cross to the entrance of the cave by a wooden gangway, pass through the narrow entrance and enter a large gallery with stalactite formations and substantial traces of bat manure. The gallery leads on for two or three hundred yards to a large chamber with a vaulted ceiling. Only experienced cave-explorers and speleologists should go beyond this point. Beyond are side-passages, and a narrow main passage with a mud floor. This suddenly drops thirty feet down a cliff to the channel of a little stream. This is the source of the Martha Brae river. Retrace your steps and take away with you the memory of a richly sculptured Jamaica of measureless caverns and sunless streams.

Montego Bay to Negril

A splendid tour can be made in a day, from Montego Bay via Negril, Savanna-la-Mar and Montpelier, but it is most enjoyable when time

Doctor's Cave beach, Montego Bay
[JAMAICA TOURIST BOARD, KINGSTON]

permits a stop-over in Negril. By arranging for this, you can escape from clock-watching and find relaxation in nature-watching, calling in at Tryall, stopping to see the old fort that commands Lucea harbour, adjusting to the leisurely pace of Negril, enjoying a picnic lunch on the beach at Bluefields, and returning to Montego Bay or going on to Mandeville and Kingston.

Leave Montego Bay by the A1 highway which runs west through Reading, (4.8 miles). At Reading a main road leading inland to Montpelier and Anchovy branches off to the left. It is best to return by this road. Continue on the Lucea road (A1) past some attractive houses by the sea, the most interesting being Wharf House, once the warehouse for the Montpelier estate when it produced sugar. At the Great River (7.4 miles) you cross from the parish of St James into mountainous Hanover and come to **Round Hill Estate**, and one of Jamaica's great hotels, which takes its name from the estate. The Round Hill Hotel stands on a circular knob of land overlooking the sea, a landmark easily identified by those arriving by plane. **Tryall**, (12.5 miles), has a hotel, an excellent golf course, and a number of private residences. The estate once produced sugar, and the old mill wheel of the sugar works has been restored. Some of the estate buildings were destroyed by the slaves during the Baptist

War of 1832. The water wheel is turned by water brought by aqueducts and stone gutters. Here, and occasionally along the road, there are reminders of the days when energy was provided by water and wind, by aqueducts, water wheels and windmills.

Mosquito Cove (17.5 miles,) is occasionally used by visiting yachts. It penetrates almost a mile inland.

Lucea (25.6 miles) is the capital of Hanover. It was once a busy sugar-port, of sufficient importance to be protected by a fort; this was erected on a promontory commanding the entrance to the harbour. It was named Fort Charlotte, and is one of the best preserved of the north coast forts. The old barracks form part of Rusea School, which provides education at secondary school level for children in the eleven to seventeen age range.

Hanover cherishes the memory of Alexander Bustamante, its most distinguished son. Sir Alexander's name was originally Clarke, and his father, Robert Clarke was an overseer on **Blenheim Estate**, which is reached by a side road from **Davis Cove** (34.1 miles). Blenheim is now a land settlement. The overseers' house has been reconstructed and is now a national monument. Continue your journey by way of Green Island and Orange Bay to Negril.

Accommodation: hotels and guest houses

The Jamaica Tourist Board publishes twice annually a list of the hotels of Jamaica, by resort area. Each hotel is placed in one of four categories, A, B, C, and D, according to the number of rooms and the rates charged. The rates quoted are provided by the hotels for the winter and summer seasons each year.

Visitors are advised to verify the rates with the hotels under consideration. Where there is any discrepancy, the applicable rate will be that posted in its rooms and reception areas.

The categories, A, B, C and D enable visitors to pick out luxury, expensive and medium range or budget hotels and guest houses. They do not indicate deficiencies in the standard of accommodation or in services provided.

In most cases capsule descriptions are provided for hotels and guest houses in resort areas. In the case of Kingston this is abbreviated, to indicate some amenities and the location.

It is advisable to check with restaurants whether reservations are required for dinner, and whether dress is casual or not. Generally the cuisine is international, with a selection of Jamaican specialities.

EP indicates no meals;

CP breakfast only;

MAP breakfast and dinner;

AP three meals;

AI all inclusive.

Check the current rate of exchange for the Jamaican dollar, since this is the currency in which the hotel bills must be paid. As things are, the current rates are much in favour of visitors from North America and Western Europe. Check also on the amount of the accommodation tax, which is according to the category of hotel, and be quite clear as to whether this is included in the rates quoted to you.

Where two persons occupy one room, occupancy will be treated as one for tax purposes. Bills and receipts issued by the hotel should show the amount charged for accommodation separately from any amount charged for any other item.

Excursions and attractions

Montego Bay is the centre of a network of attractions that reveal the island's natural beauty and the Jamaican way of life.

Look down from the mountains on to cane-fields strung out along a fringe of coastal plain and the beaches that line the coast. Visit busy plantations, stop at inland villages and townships, enjoy country Jamaica.

Variety and contrast abound. You pays your money and you takes your choice!

Appleton Estate Express

A train-ride from the Howard Cooke Highway to the home of some of Jamaica's finest rums, the Appleton distillery.

The tour is offered twice a week, on Tuesdays and Thursdays, from 8:30 a.m. to 4:45 p.m. Cost: US$50 per person.

You ride in luxurious air-conditioned coaches, partaking before departure of a continental breakfast. The ascent to the heights above Montego Bay is smooth, then green rolling pasturelands and banana

cultivations open out. At Appleton there is a fully conducted tour of the Ipswich caves and the Appleton distillery. A buffet Jamaican lunch is served in a recently constructed lounge. On the way back the train stops at Bogue Hill to allow for picture taking, and at Catadupa for the purchase of shirts and dresses.
Tel: 952-3692   P.O. Box 989, Montego Bay

Cornwall Beach is easily reached, for it borders Gloucester Avenue. Available on the beach are a bar, restaurant, changing rooms, toilet facilities, a disco and watersports. There is a lifeguard on duty daily from 9:00 a.m. to 5:00 p.m.
Cost: J$5; half-price for children.
The beach is operated by the Cornwall Beach Recreation Systems Ltd
Tel: 952-3464/3859

Croyden on the Mountains

Three times a week, on Tuesdays, Wednesdays, and Fridays, from 10:00 a.m. to 1:30 p.m., it is possible to visit this working plantation, 20 miles inland from Montego Bay, enjoy lunch . . . and join a guided tour of its diverse crops – coffee, pineapple, citrus, livestock and an aviary. Complimentary drinks made from fruits in season are served, and High Mountain Coffee.
Cost: US$35 per person. This includes pick-up from the hotel, and lunch, as well as the plantation tour.
Tel: 952-4137   P.O. Box 1348, Montego Bay

An Evening on the Great River

The Great River is about 10 miles from Montego Bay. Tours are available on Tuesdays, Thursdays, Sundays, 7:00 p.m. to 11:00 p.m. The river setting is dramatic, for the trip is made at night in fishing boats manned by expert boat men, who take their passengers up a torch-lit river to an Arawak-style village. This has an open bar, calypso band, dinner, floor-show and dancing to a live reggae band.
Cost: US $50 per person ($46.00 without transport to and from Montego Bay hotels).
The owner is Great River Productions Ltd, 42 Gloucester Avenue.
Tel: 952-5047/5097   P.O. Box 74, Reading, St James

Governor's Coach tours

This popular tour, the original train tour into the mountainous interior of Jamaica, runs from the Montego Bay Railway Station to Appleton and back. It allows for stops at mountain villages, at Catadupa to buy clothing, at Appleton to visit the distillery and sample the rum. Aboard are music and an open Jamaican bar.
Cost: US $50 per person; children half-price.
Tel: 953-2476 *or* Tour Office 952-2887   Fax: 953-2107

Greenwood Great House

The Great House, approximately 16 miles east of Montego Bay on the A1, is open to the public daily from 8:00 a.m. to 6:00 p.m. It contains authentic furnishings, as well as rare antique musical instruments and fascinating antique furniture with hidden compartments.
Cost: US $7 per person; children half-price.
P.O. Box 169, Montego Bay

Hilton High Day tour

This full day's visit to a private estate includes breakfast, a guided walking tour of the property, a drive to nearby Seaford Town for a conducted tour of the community centre, museum and school; then back to the estate for lunch (which includes roasted suckling pig, chicken or fish), complimentary drinks and mento music, as well as a tethered balloon ride up to 300 feet high if the wind conditions are favourable.
The tour is available on Tuesdays, Fridays and Sundays. Pick-up from the hotel starts from 7:00 a.m.; balloon ride at 8:00 a.m.; return to Montego Bay by 3:30 p.m.
Cost: US $46.00 per person, all inclusive; US $15.00 per person, balloon ride only.
Address: Pemco Apts, 16 East St, Montego Bay
Tel: 952-3343 (Office)   952-3642 (Home)

Jamaica Safari Village

Visit a crocodile exhibition and farm; meet Leah the lioness, watch live snakes, visit the petting zoo and bird sanctuary, call on the mongoose, join a guided natural history tour.

Safari Village is 20 miles east of Montego Bay, near Falmouth. It is open to visitors daily. The owners, Mr and Mrs Richard Cherkiss can be reached: C/o Lady Diane's Hotel.

Tel: 952-4415/5080

Cost: J$25.00 per person; children half-price (J$12.00)

Lollypop By the Sea

Lollypop beach is at Sandy Bay, just about five miles west of Montego Bay on the road to Lucea and Negril.

The tour is available once a week, on Wednesdays, 7:30 p.m. to 11:00 p.m. It includes a 15 minute glass-bottom boat-ride, a full reggae band, sea-food, jerked meats and dinner. Traditional dance groups perform kumina, reggae, limbo, basket dance and bamboo dance.

Cost: US $45 per person (inclusive round-trip transport from Montego Bay hotels); children half-price.

Address: Lollypop Beach, Sandy Bay, Hanover

Tel: 952-4121/5133/1202

Mountain Valley Rafting and Plantation tour

The tour to Lethe property, which is approximately 10 miles from Montego Bay, is available daily, 9:00 a.m. to 5:00 p.m. It takes about one hour; and with the tour 1½ hours. It includes touring a small coffee and banana plantation and rafting down to 'The Greens'. Complimentary liqueurs are served, and there is swimming in the river.

Cost: US $28.00 per raft (2 persons); US $36 per person (includes hotel transfer, lunch and raft); US $33 per person (without transfer).

Address: 31 Gloucester Avenue, Montego Bay

Tel: 952-4706

Rafting on the Martha Brae

This one-day excursion, is described on pages 112-113.

The Martha Brae river is near Falmouth. The excursions – 9 a.m. to 5 p.m. – are made daily except on public holidays.

Cost: US $30 per raft (2 persons)

The operator is River Raft Limited.
Tel: 952-0889   P.O. Box 1234, Montego Bay.

Rockland Bird Feeding Sanctuary

See page 108
Located about 7 miles from Montego Bay.
Daily, 3:15 p.m. to one hour before sundown.
Cost: J$30 per person. Children under 6 not allowed.
Operator/owner Miss Lisa Salmon.
Tel: 952-2009   P.O. Box 48, Anchory P.O.

Rose Hall Great House

See pages 110 to 111
Located 3 miles east of Montego Bay.
Daily, 9:30 a.m. to 6:00 p.m. Each guided tour lasts 30 minutes.
Cost: US$8.50 per person, US$4.00 per child.
Owner Rose Hall Development Limited.
Tel: 953-2323

Walter Fletcher Beach

Located in Montego Bay.
Open daily, 9:00 a.m. to 5:00 p.m. Lifeguard on duty.
The beach has a restaurant, changing rooms, lockers for rent, a
beauty parlour, snack counter, gift shop and boat cruises.
Cost: J$3.00 per person; J$1 per child.
Tel: 952-2044/1964

Walter Fletcher Beach Party

Fridays, 7:00 p.m. to 11.00 p.m.
Cost: US $30 per person; children half-price.
Shows feature a live reggae band. There is an open Jamaican bar,
a Jamaican dinner and a native floor show.
The operator's address is Mr Karl Young, Coconut Grove Great
House, P.O. Box 282, Ocho Rios.
Tel: 974-2619/5154

Restaurants

Montego Bay restaurants licensed by the Tourist Board are:
Brigadoon Restaurant, Queens Drive.
   P.O. Box 1340, Montego Bay.   Tel: 952-1723.
   International cuisine: specialties include conch-fish starter with
   rum-garlic sauce, smoked dolphin, lobster dishes.
Burger House, 67 City Centre Blvd   Tel: 952-3552
Cooke Goose Restaurant, Corner Harbour and Market Street
The Diplomat 9 Queens Drive   Tel: 952-3353
   International cuisine, gracious surroundings.
The Georgian House, 2 Orange Street   Tel: 952-0632
Julia's Restaurant, Bogue Hill, Reading   Tel: 951-1772
Kentucky Fried Chicken, 23 Orange Street   Tel: 952-4555
Lori's Restaurant, Holiday Village, Montego Bay
Pelican Grill And Cascade Room, Gloucester Ave   Tel: 952-3171
Pier 1, Howard Cooke Highway   Tel: 952-2452
Pork Pit, Gloucester Avenue
The Houseboat Fondue Restaurant, Montego Bay, Freeport
The Townhouse, 16 Church Street   Tel: 952-2660
The Waterfall, Gloucester Hotel, Gloucester Ave
   Jamaican food, and especially Jamaican breakfast.
The Walters, Gloucester Avenue
   Jamaican and American food; spare ribs, hamburgers.
Ice Cream Station, St James Street, (opposite Esso Station)
   Ice-creams, toppings, fruit salad, hot dogs, popcorn.
Texas Tacos, Celebration Plaza, Shop 3, Gloucester Ave
   Mexican food.

| 10 |
Negril and western Jamaica

Capture the spirit of Negril as quickly as possible after arrival.

Walk north, as if on a promenade, from any point on Long Bay toward Negril Bay and Booby Cay, and sense mind and body responding to incomparable Negril's charm by enjoying the intermingling of sophistication and natural simplicity, of the cosmopolitan and the artlessly domestic.

Or, towards evening, walk from the little town of Negril along a rampart of cliffs towards the Lighthouse, the 'Deep West' and Jamaica's most westerly fragment, Negril Point. Look west where an unbroken expanse of sea provides a stage for Negril's spectacular sunset and experience the healing power of natural beauty. Tensions ease. We accept as natural and inevitable Negril's juxtaposition of jerk chicken and French cuisine, of pizza and hair-braiders, of reggae and joggers, of horsemen on the beach offering rides and water skis, bicycles, wind surfing. No skyscrapers bisect the horizon. No towering mountains lean in on one. Freedom to explore and enjoy, this is the gift of Negril.

By day sea-water breaking on the beach sets the rhythm. By night reggae takes charge. There are reggae parties every night. The locations are usually announced by posters put up near the bridge down at the square or by criers walking up and down the beach. Daily picnics are held on enchanting Booby Cay, at the northern end of Bloody Bay, so called because whales were slaughtered there in years gone by. The picnics feature a cruise to the Cay with a stop for snorkelling on the reef, and a barbecue on the beach. Instead of hotels the little Cay boasts rondavels and bushed-out pathways instead of asphalted roads.

All day the sea beckons, offering water-sports of every kind – snorkelling, scuba-diving, deep-sea fishing, cruising, parasailing, jet skis, wind-surfing, water-skiing, and occasionally a sunset cruise. The caves at West End can be approached by sea while Xtabi and Blue Cave Castle have steps leading down to them.

Gradually, as part of the process of getting acquainted and not by deliberate effort, one becomes aware of the chief physical

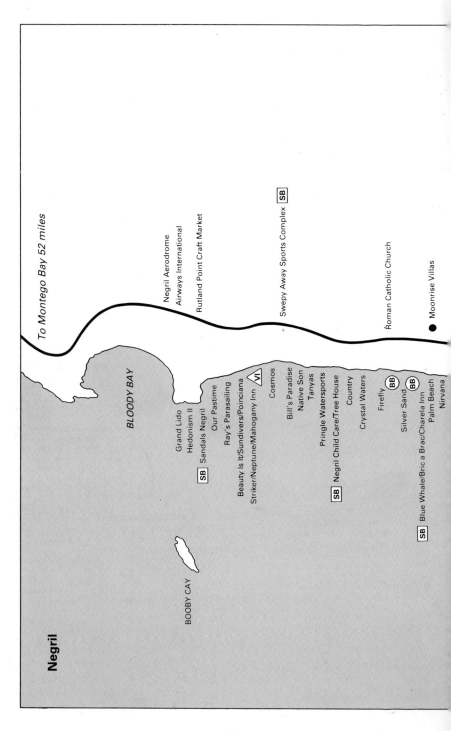

Negril

To Montego Bay 52 miles

BLOODY BAY

BOOBY CAY

Negril Aerodrome
Airways International
Rutland Point Craft Market

Grand Lido
Hedonism II
SB Sandals Negril
Our Pastime
Ray's Parasailing
Beauty Is It/Sundivers/Poinciana
Striker/Neptune/Mahogany Inn VI
Cosmos
Bill's Paradise
Native Son
Tanyas
Pringle Watersports
SB Negril Child Care/Tree House
Country
Crystal Waters
Firefly
BB Silver Sand
SB Blue Whale/Bric a Brac/Charela Inn BB
Palm Beach
Nirvana

Swepy Away Sports Complex SB

Roman Catholic Church

● Moonrise Villas

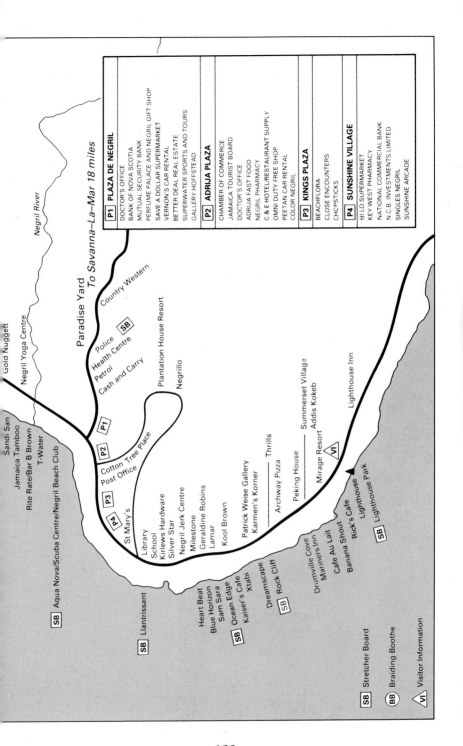

Negril River

Paradise Yard
To Savanna-La-Mar 18 miles

Gold Nuggett
Sandi San
Jamaica Tamboo
Rite Rate/Bar B Brown
T-Water
Negril Yoga Centre

SB Aqua Nova/Scuba Centre/Negril Beach Club

Country Western

Police
Health Centre **SB**
Petrol
Cash and Carry

Plantation House Resort

Negrillo

P1

P2

Cotton Tree Place
Post Office

P3

P4
St Mary's
Library
School
Kirlews Hardware
Silver Star
Negril Jerk Centre
Milestone
Geraldine Robins
Lamar
Kool Brown
Patrick Weise Gallery
Karmen's Korner
Thrills
Archway Pizza

Peking House

Summerset Village
Addis Kokeb

Mirage Resort

VI

Lighthouse Inn

Lighthouse

Rick's Cafe
Banana Shout
Cafe Au Lait
Mariners Inn
Drumville Cove

Lighthouse Park

SB

SB Liantrissant

Heart Beat
Blue Horizon
Sam Sara
Ocean Edge
Kaiser's Cafe
Xtabi
Dreamscape
Rock Cliff **SB**

SB

SB Stretcher Board
BB Braiding Boothe
VI Visitor Information

P1 PLAZA DE NEGRIL
DOCTOR'S OFFICE
BANK OF NOVA SCOTIA
MUTUAL SECURITY BANK
PERFUME PALACE AND NEGRIL GIFT SHOP
SAVE A DOLLAR SUPERMARKET
VERNON'S CAR RENTAL
BETTER DEAL REAL ESTATE
SUPERWATER SPORTS AND TOURS
GALLERY HOFFSTEAD

P2 ADRIJA PLAZA
CHAMBER OF COMMERCE
JAMAICA TOURIST BOARD
DOCTOR'S OFFICE
ADRIJA FAST FOOD
NEGRIL PHARMACY
C & E HOTEL/RESTAURANT SUPPLY
OMNI DUTY FREE SHOP
PEETAN CAR RENTAL
COLOR NEGRIL

P3 KINGS PLAZA
BEACHFLORA
CLOSE ENCOUNTERS
CHICPSTICKS

P4 SUNSHINE VILLAGE
HI LO SUPERMARKET
KEY WEST PHARMACY
NATIONAL COMMERCIAL BANK
N.C.B. INVESTMENTS LIMITED
SINGLES NEGRIL
SUNSHINE ARCADE

125

features: the country town with its central roundabout and its little bridge across Negril River, the three-mile stretch of cliffs that extend to the Lighthouse, and, northwards, Long Bay, Negril or Bloody Bay, Green Bay and Booby Cay. Inland lies the Great Morass, and beyond it Rhodes Hall Plantation, a working plantation with horseback riding, fish ponds, bananas and coconuts.

The people, visitors and locals, fit naturally into this setting; the townsfolk, proud of their new supermarket and shopping centre; the white-clad chefs in front of a jerk chicken stand, 'The Serious Chicken' in front of Sis's Green Grocery; the staff at Swept Away's sport complex, bar and eating place; Compulsion Disco at Plaza de Negril. Ask any of the locals and they will speak with pride of the way in which their town – and above all their beach – has put their once neglected parish on the world map.

Two women pirates

One of the first picnics held here was organised by a pirate, John Rackham, who was nicknamed 'Calico Jack' because of his liking for calico underwear. Calico Jack terrorised Jamaica's north coast with his frequent raids until at last he was pursued and caught by an English naval officer, Captain Barnet, in command of an armed sloop, in an unguarded moment – while holding a rum-party on the beach. He was taken to Kingston, tried, sentenced to death and hanged at Gallows Point on the Palisadoes.

Rackham's crew was captured with him. Among them were two women, Anne Bonney and Mary Read, who were dressed as men. At their trial in Spanish Town they 'pleaded their bellies, being quick with child'. Anne, who was Rackham's mistress, was finally reprieved. She had been picked up in the Bahamas. Mary Read had been brought up as a boy and had served as a trooper in Flanders during Marlborough's wars. She is reported to have died of prison fever.

The Bay had strategic value in sailing ship days, when vessels bound for England or for New Orleans were compelled by the prevailing winds to take a westerly course by way of Sav-la-mar and Negril Bay. Lady Nugent tells in her *Journal* how, in 1805, on her way back to England, they arrived 'off Negril harbour, the port of rendezvous for the fleet'. A day later 'the *Theseus* and the rest of

126

our convoy appeared in sight' . . .' Later that day

a most sudden and dreadful squall came on. We were lying in the midst of the fleet, when our cable broke, and we were in great danger of driving against a man of war that threatened to fire into us. Fortunately, however, the mate was a good seaman and he steered us safely through the ships and quite out to sea . . . As we stood out to sea another danger presented itself, from the Spanish pirates . . . Our mate, however, manoeuvred us so well that, toward evening, we had nearly got back to our former station . . .

Ten years later it was from Negril that an English expedition sailed to attack New Orleans. It is said that a Yankee trader, then in Kingston, heard that an expedition of over 6000 men, including 1000 from the 1st and 4th West India regiments was gathering at Negril under Major General Keane, the objective being to attack New Orleans. He hurriedly set sail, got to Pensacola ahead of the expedition and alerted General Andrew Jackson. True or not, the expedition was defeated.

A sampler of good things

Wherever you go, a feast of good things awaits you – representative of Jamaican and international cuisine, and of the culinary skills of chefs expert in their particular area. The list that follows is no more than a sampler that indicates the range and diversity of offerings:

All-inclusive dining

    Grand Lido
    Hedonism II
    Negril Inn
    Sandals Negril
    Swept Away

Snorkelling by Negril's West End *overleaf*
[JAMAICA TOURIST BOARD, NEW YORK]

French

Cafe au Lait, West End Road
Charela Inn, Negril Beach

German

LTU Pub – West End Road
Negril Lighthouse Inn, West End Road

Italian

Archway Pizza
Sweet Bite Cafe
Silver Star Cafe
Tambo

Oriental (Chinese)

Chop Stix, King's Plaza
Country, Negril Beach
Negril Yacht Club, West End Road
Peking House, West End Road

Vegetarian

Country, Negril Beach
Hungry Lion, West End Road
Paradise Yard, Nonpareil Road
Swept Away, Negril Beach
Tanya's, Negril Beach

Pastry and patties

Bread Basket, Town Plaza
Fair Flakes, West End Road
Jah Bahs High-powered Ethiopian Health Centre, West End
  Road
Sugar Shack, Rock Cliff, West End Road

The North-western Coast – Negril-Lucea-Tryall

Negril and Montego Bay are the best places from which to explore the island's north-west coast, with its many charming inlets and caves, its many reminders of the island's sugar-age and of the imperial wars of the eighteenth century.

We will start from Negril Town and head first for Lucea, capital of the parish, and known to all Jamaicans for 'Lucea yam', one of the most delectable of white yams, light and floury.

Lucea, a small town of 3500 people, is coming back to life after a long period of neglect. It stands on the western side of an almost land-locked harbour, a great advantage in the days when the surrounding sugar-estates shipped their sugar and rum from this port. Fort Charlotte, now in ruins, commands the entrance to the harbour and gives proof of Lucea's importance when sugar was King.

Of special interest is Rusea's School, which occupies a part of the barracks that were built to house the forces that manned the fort. The school bears the name of a French refugee, Martin Rusea, who

> *in grateful recollection of the hospitality manifested toward him in the colony, left by his Will dated 13 July 1764, all his real and personal estate for the establishment of a school in the parish of Hanover.*

The Will was disputed by relatives for some years, then a trust was set up with the proceeds of the estate, and Jamaica gained one of its best known schools.

The Parish Church contains a marble monument to Simon Clarke, 'a man of elegant manners and classical education' who sought, we are told, to restore his fallen family to its ancient splendour. Concerning his effort Wright and White, in *Exploring Jamaica* (now out of print) wrote that

> *the fallen family may allude to the story that the 5th baronet, an officer in the navy, was transported to Jamaica for highway robbery, but more probably to the fact that the 6th baronet, Sir Simon's father, wasted his fortune in a vain search for rich veins of precious ore in the island's central highlands.*

Tryall, our goal, lies twelve miles beyond Lucea on the highway to

Montego Bay.

Ruined forts and windmills tell a story of fallen fortunes. Tryall, in contrast, demonstrates how imagination and capital combined can transform ruined greatness into a profitable asset. Some thirty years ago an American syndicate bought the property, used the old Great House as the nucleus around which to build an attractive modern hotel, put in a now internationally famous golf course where sugar-cane once grew, repaired the mill wheel of the old sugar works, brought water from the Flint River by aqueducts and stone gutters, set the old wheel turning again and made it a dramatic logo of the new Tryall.

The South-west Coast and Western Highlands
Negril-Savanna la Mar, Montego Bay

For a delightful excursion drive from Negril by way of the south-west coast to Savanna-la-Mar, then turn north at Ferris Cross and enjoy highland Jamaica, some of it rolling cattle-country and some less hospitable looking, with jagged limestone crags and scattered peasant holdings.

Leaving Negril, travel east by way of Sheffield and Little London to Savanna-la-Mar, eighteen miles from Negril and thirty-three miles from Montego Bay by the B8. Savanna-la-Mar, often called Sav-la-Mar for short, is the capital of the parish of Westmoreland most of which, in contrast to Hanover, lies on a fertile alluvial plain and has several cattle ranches.

Founded in 1730, Sav-la-Mar became an important and busy port that served the inland sugar estates. Nature treated the town roughly in its early years. When it was eleven years old a hurricane bore down upon it, and, wrote the historian Bryan Edwards, 'the sea bursting its ancient limits overwhelmed that unhappy town and swept it to instant destruction'. The treatment was repeated thirty-two years later; another hurricane brought disaster:

the sea rose, a mighty wave swept up the beach for nearly a mile and, as it retired, left two ships and a schooner stranded among the trees.

Having survived the perils of youth, Sav-la-Mar grew up around Great George Street, described by naturalist Philip Gosse as:

a broad long street that constitutes the town. Most of the
houses are shops, or stores as they are called in the American
manner, each . . . with an open piazza in front, three or four
yards wide, in which the various goods are displayed, and
in which the owner may commonly be seen with a friend or
customer, seated on chairs, the feet often on another chair
(this too is in American fashion) discussing the amenities of
a cigar or a glass of malt . . .

Gosse, apparently, did not care for American fashions, but
Jamaica's sugar-ports had frequent and close contacts with the USA
and Sav-la-Mar was no exception. Abraham Lopez, for example, a
local merchant, was the local agent for a leading Rhode Island
merchant, Aaron Lopez.

Sav-la-Mar was the home of a Church of England priest, the Revd
Henry Clarke (1820 – 1907), who identified himself with the great
mass of Jamaicans, to the displeasure of the planters and Anglican
clergy. At the time of the Morant Bay rising he protested strongly
to the Anti-Slavery Society in England about the illegal execution
of George William Gordon, and prophesied that Gordon would one
day be honoured with a national monument. Henry Clarke took the
lead in founding the Westmoreland Building Society, now the
National Building Society. His family continued the tradition of
public service through the late Edith Clarke, author and social
worker, and Eric Clarke, formerly a Custos of the parish.

Manning's School, on the main road west of the Building Society's
office on the corner of Beckford and Barracks Street, owes its
beginnings to a Westmoreland planter, Thomas Manning, who left
thirteen slaves, land and the produce of a pen and cattle to endow
a free school. The school was founded in 1738, twenty-eight years
after Manning's death. It has been greatly enlarged and now, like
Rusea's holds an honoured place in the history of Jamaican education.

From Sav-la-Mar drive east along the A2 to Ferris Cross (5 miles)
and turn left through Whithorn (4 miles) to Haddo, home of Charles
Stewart, one of Jamaica's many prophets, who was known as 'the
prophet of Haddo'. He attracted a large following by his predictions.
He built a shrine in the hills and a balm-yard. The building is easily
recognised by a white flag on a pole, often with a display of other

flags also, where a 'balm-yard man' or 'balm-yard woman' practises herb-healing, folk-medicine and either obeah or myal healing, both these being against the law. Bush teas and 'fever baths' made with collections of herbs or 'bush' are essential parts of the process.

Knockalva, three miles beyond Haddo, is an agricultural training centre for youths of fifteen to nineteen. **Montpelier**, twenty miles from Sav-la-Mar and just over eleven from Montego Bay, is one of the largest cattle properties in Jamaica.

Montpelier, Haddo and Mount Carey are counterpoints in the history of Jamaica. They symbolise the imported and the indigenous, scientific technology and folk-beliefs. The three places point to different, even opposed forces, which shaped Jamaica's way of life; they also point to the future, to Jamaica's capability for drawing on external sources of technology and capital without weakening its sense of independence.

For one hundred and sixty years, from 1752 to 1912, Montpelier belonged to the Ellis family. This Jamaica connection dated back to the period of Charles II of Britain, when John Ellis came to the island and patented Ellis Caymanas near Spanish Town. A descendant, Charles Rose Ellis (1771 – 1845), was an absentee proprietor who lived in England and was one of the leaders of the West Indian interests there. He was raised to the peerage as Lord Seaford. After sugar prices fell in the 1840s, Montpelier switched to cattle, and was one of the pioneers in importing Mysore and Zebu cattle from India. These were able to withstand drought and heat. Experimental breeding was continued throughout the years and became a feature of the Montpelier-Shettlewood estates.

By chance, the Ellis family also had a hand in importing guinea grass, which provided better feed for the cattle. The captain of a slave ship brought in for Chief Justice Ellis some rare African birds and a bag of the seed on which they fed. The birds died. The bag with the seed was shaken out and forgotten. Some time afterwards the cattle were seen to be gathering at a particular place and enjoying an unknown grass. The African seed, guinea grass, was remembered and the place was fenced in; the grass spread and Jamaica gained a grass that for a long period sustained its cattle industry.

From Montpelier a road leads to Cambridge and Seaford Town, twelve miles away. The village is named after Lord Seaford, who gave five hundred acres of partially cleared land for settling a number of Germans who were brought in after emancipation to settle as peasant farmers. About two hundred and fifty of them settled but they had a difficult time. Some died, others emigrated. Today Seaford Town is a community of fair-skinned, small farmers of German origin.

Mount Carey Baptist Church, twenty-two miles from Sav-la-Mar and just over nine from Montego Bay, speaks of the struggle for emancipation and the work of Thomas Burchell, whose name is recorded on an obelisk, and William Knibb. After the abolition of slavery in 1834 Thomas Burchell made his home here. Like the Webb Memorial Church in Falmouth and the Burchell Memorial Baptist Church in Montego Bay, Mount Carey is a reminder of the struggle of the people and of the missionaries to achieve freedom. Bethel Town, five miles from Mount Carey, is one of the free villages which Burchell founded after emancipation.

The prophet of Haddo should not be dismissed as 'superstitious' or 'mad'. He is one of a large company of shepherds and shepherdesses, preachers and prophets, balm-yard men and balm-yard women who became aware of, and sought to minister to, deep spiritual needs in the society. They had a sense of mission. Some were Messianic leaders to whom the folk immediately responded. Mount Carey, on the one hand, symbolises the struggle for, and achievement of, freedom. It symbolises also a blend of 'native Baptist' with Christian missionary teaching and guidance. Montpelier, on the other hand, points to the value of external influences and knowledge for improving agricultural technology and strengthening the island's economy.

| 11 |
Ocho Rios and its neighbours

Each cove and inlet has its own individuality. The family likeness is there – coconut palms reminding us of Mark Twain's description of a palm-tree as a feather duster transfixed by lightning, breadfruit and mango trees, inshore waters in rainbow colours, gleaming white sand. The family likeness cannot efface or mask the individuality of each strip of north-coast beach, its own special setting of flowering shrubs, of pastureland and headland. The coast has not been prettied up nor wrapped in cellophane packages. The earth is good and earthy, the sea good and salty, and the trees dig their roots vigorously into the soil. At any moment a deep Jamaican voice might break the silence with a ribald song about Matilda whose garments came asunder.

Ocho Rios, the centre of a far-spreading network of resorts, stands on a strip of coast that the Spanish colonists of the sixteenth century called Las Chorreras, the Waterfalls. Now, four centuries later, those travelling by road from Ocho Rios to St Ann's Bay can see why the Spanish colonists spoke of 'Waterfalls'.

But why should they have called Ocho Rios 'eight rivers'? Some dispute that theory and suggest that the English mispronounced 'Las Chorreras', transforming it into Ocho Rios. Whatever the origin, Jamaicans have affectionately compressed it into 'Ochy'.

Before focusing on Ocho Rios and its neighbours, let us look at the coast from a vantage point on one of the roads that leads from the coast up the escarpment to Moneague, Claremont and Brown's Town.

One crystal morning I stood looking from a vantage point on the Chalky Hill road, tracing the contoured pattern from the fringe of offshore reef across the rim of plain to the upland terraces. The inevitable goat was there, tethered by the side of the road, for that is common property and why should the public grass not provide food for a private entrepreneur? It was so clear a morning that I

Ocho Rios Bay *opposite* [JAMAICA TOURIST BOARD, KINGSTON]

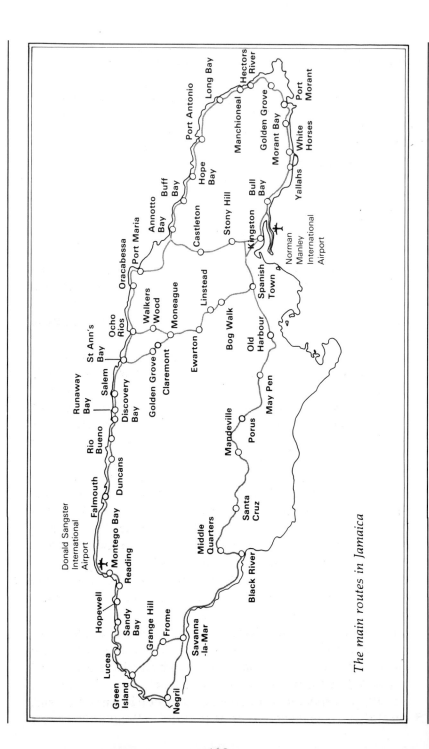

The main routes in Jamaica

almost persuaded myself the clouds on the distant horizon were the mountains of Oriente Province in Cuba.

Suddenly I became aware of someone approaching. It was an elderly woman, bony, as finely chiselled as an old pimento tree.

She spoke very quietly. 'Pretty, pretty for true, thank Massa God. I live here from when I was a little child and I never get tired of this. You know, I don't have no money, but this belongs to me, to me and Massa God. Pretty for true.' She asked for nothing but the companionship of sharing this beauty.

General information

Ocho Rios is on the north coast of Jamaica, midway between Montego Bay in the west (67 miles) and Port Antonio in the east (67 miles). It is sixty miles from Kingston, which lies to the southeast. A small country town, with a population of seven thousand, it stands on a semi-circular bay which has a deep water pier with berthing for two ships. The Reynolds Jamaica Mines Company ships bauxite from Ocho Rios to the United States. Their installations for storage and shipping are toward the western part of the bay.

As the map shows, it is easy to reach Ocho Rios from almost any part of Jamaica. Trans-Jamaica, Wings Jamaica and Jamaica Air Taxi use the Boscobel Airport, which is twenty minutes from the centre of town. The highway from Kingston, the A1, goes by way of Spanish Town and the Bog Walk Gorge to Moneague, where there is a junction with the A3. The shorter and more scenic route is by the A3 from Moneague by way of the Fern Gully to Ocho Rios.

The route from Montego Bay is by the A1, through Discovery Bay and St Ann's Bay by the A3, which continues beyond Ocho Rios, Port Maria and Annotto Bay to Port Antonio.

A network of roads links Ocho Rios with the towns and villages of Central Jamaica. There will be a description of some of these in the section on tours and excursions.

Ocho Rios is a happy place, secure in itself. It is not burdened with being the capital of a parish, like St Ann's Bay, seven miles to the west. It is neither a commercial nor an industrial centre, though Reynolds Jamaica Mines is only twelve miles away, at Lydford. It is a large resort but it is not dominated by hotels. They are strung out along forty miles of coast from the Sandals Dunn's River Resort to the west to Oracabessa, twenty-five miles to the east. The visual impact of a luxury development such as the Shaw Park Corniche, possibly the finest of its kind in Jamaica, or of the hotels and expensive villas that line the coast, is diminished by the fact that they all fit into a landscape of gardens; and these gardens 'belong'. They are not so manicured as to appear artificial. Jamaicans also belong here. They welcome visitors but they are the hosts.

The impact of Ocho Rios is immediate and affirmative without being assertive or aggressive. Pause at the wayside stalls that line the road from Pineapple Place to Jamaica Inn, or at the market in Ocho Rios, or at the little shops that sell Jamaica patties, curried goat, jerk pork, jerk chicken, sweet potato pone, and gizadas (which are pastry shells filled with sweetened grated coconut). Home-made ginger beer performs the double function of calming the stomach and refreshing the body; at Christmas time, try the appetiser made from sorrel flavoured with ginger. Try roast corn on the cob and beef soup or goat-head soup. The indigenous is everywhere. It is not swept under the counter.

Give some time to the carvings especially. Most Jamaicans are descendants of African peoples, predominantly of the Akan-Ashanti people of Ghana and of the Ibo people of Nigeria. These, in common

Dunn's River Falls
[JAMAICA TOURIST BOARD, KINGSTON]

with so many other African peoples, have a long tradition of wood-carving. Haiti never forgot it. Jamaica did. A revival of spirit came with the national movement of the 1930s when Jamaica began to express itself in music, the dance, painting, carving and literature. There is an almost confusing profusion of work. The output is uneven, but the discerning eye will find work of quality.

In contrast to Negril, which stands alone, Ocho Rios is the heart of an extensive resort area, of a vigorous dynamic system extending from Discovery Bay east to Port Maria, and inland to include country towns such as Moneague, Claremont and Brown's Town.

Ocho Rios is not built around a central square or large business area. It flows along both sides of the highway from the Reynolds Bauxite port to the west to Sans Souci Hotel in the direction of the White River. Houses, shops and booths, cars, pedestrians in shorts, swimming trunks, bikinis, a wild assortment of hats and bikes, generate a holiday feeling. There are two constellations of shops along this pulsing artery, the Ocean Village Shopping Centre and, farther to the east, the Pineapple Shopping Centre.

A sampler of restaurants

The many hotels in the Ocho Rios region are the pace setters when it comes to all-inclusive dinners. There is a wide choice and visitors are advised to study the list of hotels produced by the Jamaica Tourist Board. It will give more up-to-date information than can any guide book. Catering, as they do, to an international clientele, they maintain high standards in every respect.

The list given here is a sampler indicating the range of choice available in Ocho Rios outside of the hotels.

Chinese

China Town, Main Street

Chinese and international

The Ruins, DaCosta Drive

Italian

Le Gourmand, Coconut Grove Shopping Centre
Piccolo Mondo, Boscobel

Jamaican and general

Beach Bowl, Ocean Village
Carib Inn, Main Street
Palm Beach, Ocean Village
Parkway, DaCosta Drive

Seafood

Glen's Restaurant, Tower Isle
Lobster Pot, Main Street
Trade Winds, Main Street

Pasta and specialties

Burger King, Main Street
Kentucky Fried Chicken, Main Street
Shakey's Pizza Parlour, Main Street
The King's Arms (old English pub), Harmony Hall

Excursions and tours

Brimmer Hall Estate

Take the north coast road from Ocho Rios by way of Couples Hotel
(3½ miles), across the Rio Nuevo (5.9 miles) where the English
defeated Yssassi, by way of the Golden Head Hotel, through
Oracabessa seaport, passing Golden Eye, home of the late Ian
Fleming, to Port Maria, 19 miles. Continue beyond the General
Hospital, then turn right on to the road to Baileys Vale and Brimmer
Hall which is two miles away. The estate organises tractor-drawn
jitney tours three times daily of a 700-acre banana and coconut
estate, and the Great House; bar and swimming pool are available.
Eating House with Jamaican dishes for lunch; well-stocked souvenir

shops; local carvings, paintings on sale. The cost of the tour is US$12 per person.

Calypso Rafting

A 45-minute raft-ride, this costs US$25 per raft (two persons) down the picturesque White River. Stop for a swim in cool mountain waters. Complimentary drinks.

Circle 'B' Farm

Near Priory, on the outskirts of St Ann's Bay. Walking guided tour of about two hours of a model Jamaican small farm with a diversified operation. Welcome rum or fruit punch, fruits in season, and a native buffet lunch. Tour and fruit plate, US$9; tour and lunch, US$18. Mr Bob Miller, a champion farmer, will personally conduct farm tours for special groups with a real interest in agriculture. For this, appointments are necessary. Address: Liberty District, Priory, St Ann. Tel. 972-2988.

Evening on the White River
[JAMAICA TOURIST BOARD, KINGSTON]

Dunns River Park and Falls

Deservedly popular for their natural beauty and for the fun they provide. The Dunns River cascades six hundred feet down a series of limestone terraces and ledges to a wide beach of white sand, so one can mix freshwater and salt, climb the falls or clamber down them from the Park, and swim in the warmer sea. Open daily, 8:00 a.m. to 5:00 p.m. Cost: J$21, includes climbing the falls and use of picnic park, changing rooms, toilet facilities, and picnic park on other side of road, with restaurant.

Evening on the White River

Features a boat-ride up a torch-lit river, Jamaican dinner, open Jamaican bar, live reggae music, native floor show and dancing. Sundays and Tuesdays. Cost: US$32 per person. Contact Coconut Grove Great House, Tel. 974-2619.

Firefly

The late Noel Coward's one-bedroom hilltop eyrie at Grants Pen, in hills above Port Maria. Guided tour of house and grounds daily (9:00 a.m. to 5:00 p.m.): J$10 per adult; $2.50 children.

Harmony Hall

This gracious Victorian building, skilfully restored and decorated with ginger-bread fretwork, houses one of the best art galleries on the north coast. It includes the work of some of Jamaica's internationally known artists, such as David Boxer, Everald Brown, Kapo, Chris Gonzalez, Judy MacMillan and others.

The Art Gallery alone makes Harmony Hall worth a visit. The main Gallery holds regular exhibits of group and one-man shows while other rooms contain constantly changing works. In addition, a fine collection of carvings, *objets d'art*, hand-made figurines, prints and posters are on sale.

To cap it all, the King's Arms invites visitors to enjoy the atmosphere of an old English pub.

Prospect Plantation tour
[JAMAICA TOURIST BOARD, KINGSTON]

Lilyfield Great House

At Bamboo, St Ann. This tour features a four-hour tour including the Green Grotto Caves, then Kaiser in Discovery Bay to view bauxite operations there; continues to Brown's Town market where fruits can be bought. On to Lilyfield for lunch, a brief history of Great House and also instructions on how to prepare Jamaican dishes. Non-alcoholic drink offered on arrival at Great House.

Prospect Plantation tour

Within a few minutes of the centre of Ocho Rios; jitney tour of Jamaica's economic crops in their natural setting – bananas, pineapples, sugar-cane, cocoa, coffee, limes and pimento. View the White River Gorge, Jamaica's first hydro-electric power station and commemorative trees planted by world-famous visitors.
Monday to Saturdays at 10:30 a.m., 2:00 p.m., 3:30 p.m.
Sundays at 11:00 a.m., 1.30 p.m., 3.30 p.m.
Cost: US$10.00.
Contact: Estate Tour Services Limited, Tel: 974-2058.

Prospect Miniature Golf Course

Open daily, 9:00 a.m. to 4:30 p.m. US$4.00 adults, children half-price.

Puerto Seco Beach

At Discovery Bay; open daily 9:00 a.m. to 5:00 p.m. (except on Good Fridays). Has bar and restaurant, toilet facilities, limited water sports. Cost: J$4:00 adults, J$2.00 children.

Reggae Lobster Party

At Coconut Grove Great House, Ocho Rios. Thursdays 7:00 p.m. to 11:00 p.m. Cost: US$30.00 per person. Features reggae music by Jah Reggae Band; native floor show; open Jamaican bar, dinner.

Rio Bueno

Rio Bueno – Joe James Gallery, Lobster Bowl Restaurant, Tel: 953-2392. Rio Bueno, on the coast road from Montego Bay to Ocho Rios, 30 miles from each, gets much less attention than it merits, largely because it has no sandy beaches. This may have been the horseshoe-shaped bay where Columbus first landed in Jamaica, and which he called Puerto Bueno. The port came to life in the last century, its wharf busy with the bustle of loading sugar and rum. Houses and shops of stone lined the street. At the entrance to the village are the ruins of Fort Dundas. One of the stones by the front gateway bears the date 1778. Near the fort, in a walled churchyard, is a small, beautifully proportioned Anglican church, St Marks. Inside the church is a colour print of Rio Bueno as the artist, Joseph Kidd, saw it in the 1830s.

A side road, unpaved after the first mile, leads from Rio Bueno to Bryan Castle, three miles inland, residence of the greatest historian of the Caribbean during the colonial period, Bryan Edwards. His *History, Civil and Commercial of the West Indian Colonies (1793)* went into five editions and was translated into French and German. The work is much sought after by book collectors.

Joe James, an English artist who has adopted Jamaica, built his home and gallery here. He supervises an art centre that produces sculpture and wood-carvings. Joe James' work includes sketches, oil paintings and carvings. Meals are served in the Lobster Bowl Restaurant, either inside or on a patio by the water: specialties include lobster, fish, steak, turtle steak.

Shaw Park Botanical Gardens

The garden features a waterfall, tropical trees, flowering shrubs such as bougainvillea, oleander, shower of gold. The Gardens contain interesting examples of various varieties of ferns and tree-ferns.
　　Open daily 9:00 a.m. to 5:00 p.m. Cost: US$3.50 adults; children half-price.
　　Jamaica has more than five hundred species of ferns. Fern lovers will find an excellent collection in the Herbarium of the Institute of Jamaica, in Kingston. A Jamaica variety, the Sword Fern, was taken to America in 1793. Forty years later a new variety suddenly appeared in a greenhouse near Boston; since then the Boston fern has given rise to more than two hundred different forms.

Columbus at St Ann's Bay

Arawak Jamaica came face to face with Europe when Columbus landed at St Ann's Bay – his Santa Gloria – on 5 May, 1494. The contact was brief. His voyage was no more than a reconnaissance to determine the size and shape of the island. He stopped briefly at St Ann's Bay, Discovery Bay, Montego Bay, and later at Portland Bight on the South Coast, then returned to his base in Hispaniola.
　　The second visit was unintended and undesired. In 1509, on his way back from exploring the Central American coast, he was forced to stop at St Ann's Bay. His two caravels, riddled with worms and battered by storms, were sinking. To reach Hispaniola was impossible. 'The Lord,' he said, 'brought me to land by a miracle.'
　　The Admiral was marooned at St Ann's Bay for a year, waiting for help from Santo Domingo. The Arawaks in near-by villages supplied him with food, but at one time, angry at the cruelty of some of the Spaniards, they refused to continue doing this. Columbus, from his copy of the Astronomic Calendar, knew that a total eclipse of the moon was due so he summoned the Arawak chiefs and told them that if they refused him food his God would take away the

moon from the sky that evening. When the eclipse began the terrified Indians promised to mend their ways and begged Columbus to intercede for them. At the appropriate time the Admiral prayed and the moon gradually reappeared.

After a year of waiting, help came from Santo Domingo. So it came about that Columbus spent a longer time in Jamaica than in any other part of the Caribbean save Hispaniola.

A Columbus pilgrimage

This decade witnesses world-wide celebrations of Columbus' 1492 voyage of discovery and exploration. It is an appropriate time to visit Seville, the site of the first Spanish capital of Jamaica, on the western limits of St Ann's Bay. The town, Sevilla Nueva, was founded in 1510, at the spot where Columbus made his first landfall. By the side of the road, at the entrance to the estate, stands the Columbus monument. It portrays the Admiral in the dress of a Spanish grandee of the period. Inscribed bronze plaques on the pedestal picture the three caravels of the explorer's first voyage of 1492. The monument, the work of a Roman sculptor Michele Guerisi, was cast in Columbus' native town of Genoa. Built into the Catholic shrine which stand a little distance up the driveway are stones from the old Spanish church at Seville. The zeal and leadership of two Catholic priests, Father Neil Donahue, SJ and Father Ray Sullivan, brought about the erection of the monument and the shrine.

Jamaican orchids *opposite* [CAROLINE LEE]

| 12 |
Port Antonio, the Rio Grande and Bath Spa

General information

Port Antonio, capital of the parish of Portland, is on the north-east coast of Jamaica, almost at the point where the coast swings sharply south. It has a population of 10 000, about one-tenth that of the whole parish.

By air Port Antonio is seventeen minutes from the Tinson Pen airport in Kingston. As the crow flies it is twenty-two miles away but the Blue Mountain range intervenes, so travellers by road have to go around or over the barrier. One road follows the coast by way of Manchioneal and Hectors River to Holland Estate where it turns west toward Kingston by way of Morant Bay. The distance is seventy-seven miles, the time two and a half hours.

The other popular route is by the A4, commonly called the Junction Road, west to Annotto Bay, and then by the A3, which follows the valley of the Wag Water, bobbing and weaving for some twenty miles until it comes into open country; then by way of Stony Hill to Kingston. This is a shorter route, sixty miles, and the road is well-surfaced, but the corkscrew stretch in the middle calls for caution.

A third route follows the A4 to Buff Bay, then turns left on to the B1, and climbs up to Hardwar Gap, 4000 feet high. Having passed through the Gap, it descends by way of Newcastle to Papine and Kingston. The distance is sixty miles, but much of the twenty-three miles between Buff Bay and Hardwar Gap is rough going. Visitors who use this road or who drive up any of the Portland valleys soon see how mountainous a parish Portland is. Two-thirds of it, 240 square miles, is more than 1000 feet above sea-level; one third is more than 3000 feet high.

As a result, Portland is less densely populated than most Jamaican parishes. Also, it was never a sugar parish. The chief products are bananas and coconuts, with some cattle. The mountain slopes face the north-east trade winds, which sweep in heavy with rainclouds

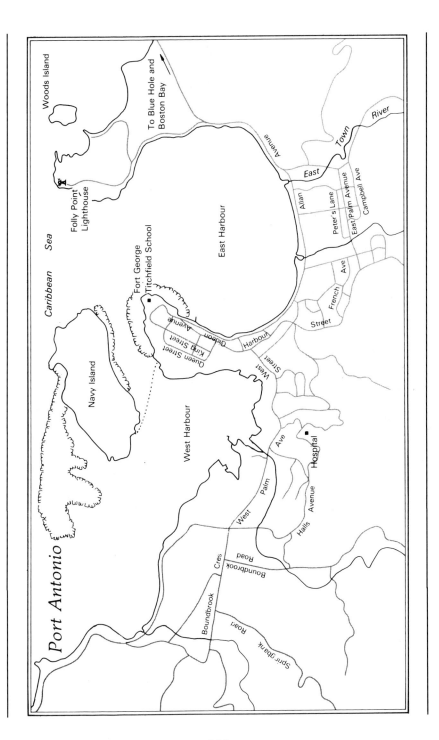

making the high mountains and valleys the wettest part of Jamaica, feeding streams and tributaries into the Rio Grande, the Swift River, the Buff Bay River and other Portland rivers. It is drier along the coast. Port Antonio has an average of twenty-four sunny days a month. When the rain comes it falls heavily, then it clears and the sun returns.

Superlatives are always suspect, but Port Antonio's twin harbours deserve them. They are best seen from a vantage point such as the Bonnie View Hotel. The road up climbs sharply but is quite safe. From the hotel grounds it is possible to pick out Upper Titchfield on a narrow promontory that separates East Harbour from West Harbour; the old military barracks of Fort George and the Titchfield School; Navy Island, a mini-edition of Crusoe's island, covered with coconut trees; and Lower Titchfield which runs west along the waterfront, with wharves, shops, Town Hall and market. The deep blue of the West Harbour in its emerald setting of palms, the unspoiled perfection of Navy Island guarding the channel and providing the eye with a near horizon, and the sea-green of the shallower East Harbour make this one of the loveliest harbours to be found anywhere.

Mystery and grandeur are the words for Port Antonio and its surroundings, in spite of the fact that parts of the town are shabby and down-at-heel; that the galvanised tin roofs of some of the shops and houses are rusty; and that the streets of the town are mean in their proportions. The natural beauty gives a charm even to these; and mystery and grandeur remain the words.

The mountains set the mood. Portlanders are mountain-loving people, though steep hillsides break the back of a farmer. 'To reach my district,' said a Portland woman, 'you have to travel five miles of continuous hill with the houses jotted in between.' She was one of the Maroon people who live around Moore Town. Their story adds to the mystery of the mountains. To this day they are credited with special skills in folk-medicine, in the use of healing leaves to make 'Maroon blister'; and there are stories of how they used vines and withes, 'Maroon wiss-wiss' to camouflage themselves, and of how they used sharp-pointed wooden lances, 'Maroon lance' in fighting and hunting.

As a child born in a Methodist manse near Manchioneal, I still recall the excitement and fear with which I listened to 'Cookie' as she told stories about the Maroons, how they hunted wild pigs in the mountains and cooked 'jerk pork'; how they could find their way through the John Crow mountains; how they talked to each other on the abeng or bull horn; how they had the power of appearing and disappearing. She told also how Nanny, one of the Maroon leaders, held out against the English soldiers; how she could heal those Maroons who were wounded; how she absorbed the bullets of the English soldiers in her capacious backside. She told how, even now, at Nanny Town, white birds roost in the trees at evening time, birds such as no one ever sees by day, for they are the ghosts of the Nanny Town dead.

Portland offers beauty that is at times almost overwhelming. Those who discover it usually return. It also offers a challenge. To get to know the land and its people one needs to go into the valleys of the Rio Grande and Swift River, to visit Millbank and Moore Town, Golden Vale, Skibo, Coopers Hill and the upper reaches of the Back River. Guides are available for those who wish to go into less frequented country.

This combination of natural beauty and challenge, of mystery and grandeur, captivated Errol Flynn. He fell in love with Portland, bought Navy Island and Comfort Castle Estate, where his widow Patrice Wymore still lives, and popularised rafting on the Rio Grande. The older people who knew him loved him. 'He was a kind man,' they will tell you.

Tours and excursions

The Rio Grande and Moore Town Rafting starts at Berridale, but it is well worth driving first to Moore Town. The Road leads from Port Antonio through Fellowship (four miles), Golden Vale, and then along a high cliff overlooking the river. Pause to wonder at the glory of Blue Mountain Peak, and then proceed to Moore Town. To the east are the John Crow Mountains. They have an average height of just over 2000 feet, but they have rarely been crossed because the higher part is a waterless plateau of sharp honeycomb limestone. The range divides the Rio Grande valley from the east coast.

Blue Lagoon *overleaf* [JAMAICA TOURIST BOARD, KINGSTON]

153

Moore Town, named after Governor Henry Moore (1760 – 62), is on the banks of the Rio Grande. It was settled by the Maroons who waged a long guerilla war against the British in the eighteenth century. Those who wish to visit Moore Town should seek the help of the Tourist Board office in Port Antonio, so that their leader, the Colonel, can be notified in advance. The great festival of the year at Moore Town is the celebration in honour of Nanny, who is a national hero; the abeng horns, coromantee drums and dances fill the day with sound, and the old stories and legends are retold.

Having visited Moore Town it is worth returning to Berridale to embark on a rafting expedition. The raft is of bamboo, four feet wide, 40 feet long, sturdy, with a raised seat for two toward the back. The river captain stands at the front using a long pole to guide the raft through rapids and quiet stretches, passing banana plantations, coconut trees, through the Tunnel of Love – a narrow passage between high cliffs – for eight miles to the Rafter's Rest at Burlington on St Margaret's Bay.

On this trip of half-a-day it is noticeable that there are no Great Houses, no sugar factories, no spreading fields of sugar-cane, no plantations, just patches and fields of bananas and other food crops. This is the country of the Portland smallholders who gave Jamaica its banana industry, growing on their patches of land the bananas that Captain Baker, founder of the United Fruit Company, and his successors bought and took to the United States.

Fishing and scenic tours

Port Antonio is a popular centre for deep-sea fishing. Large marlin have been taken: wahoo, tarpon, snook, snapper, jack fish and barracuda. In the higher waters of the Rio Grande, Swift and Spanish rivers there are mountain mullet, hognose mullet and drummer. Those keen on fresh-water and deep-sea fishing should consult with the Jamaica Tourist Board.

Blue Lagoon or Blue Hole Seven miles from Port Antonio on A3 coast road. Signs point the way from the main road down to the beach, to a restaurant and bar overlooking the lagoon, a large circular expanse of startlingly blue water, 180 feet deep. Visitors are admitted between 10:00 a.m. and 10:00 p.m. daily. Facilities include

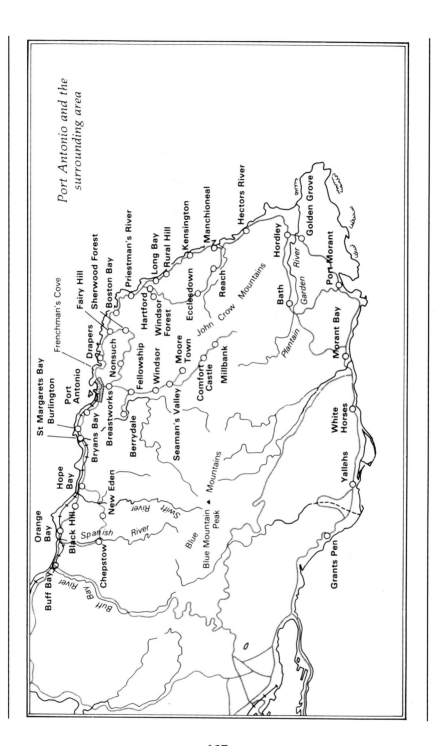

Port Antonio and the surrounding area

water-skiing in the bay, scuba-diving off the reef, trips in a glass-bottomed boat, rental of waterskiing and diving equipment. On leaving, if the light allows, continue a short way along the A3 east, then stop and look down on the lagoon, intensely blue in a setting of dark-green trees.

Boston Beach   Ten miles east of Port Antonio, it is protected by an off-shore reef. It has an excellent beach of fine sand, and is ideal for a swim and picnic.

Scenic Tours include:

(a) driving from **Port Antonio** to **Swift River**, and **Mount Hermon** to **Chepstow**, through **Skibo** and back by way of **Black Hill**;

(b) by way of the **Park Mountain** road and **Golden Vale** for a magic combination of river and mountain scenery;

(c) **Somerset Falls**, ten miles west of Port Antonio, past Hope Bay on the A4. The Daniels River plunges down a narrow gorge bordered with tropical rainforests. There are picnic places and bathing in cool, deep rock pools, on the upper levels of the river.

(d) The **Caves of Nonsuch**. The signs point right, away from the A3. This side road leads for six miles through small villages, to the Caves. It is possible to continue along the road which twists and turns back to Port Antonio.

The East Coast and Bath Spa   Take the A3 east, past San San Bay, Frenchman's Cove, the Blue Lagoon (seven miles) and Boston Beach (10 miles). The coastal plain is much narrower, for the sombre John Crow Mountains press down on the coast, leaving little elbow-room.

Gradually the aspect of the land changes from lush tropical to arid and windswept. From Priestman's River, we drive along a windy rock-bound coast where the trees lean inland under the pressure of the trade winds; past Long Bay, with its fine beach and lively sea; by way of Manchioneal whose name is a reminder of an early botanist's description of the machineel tree as 'full of a very fiery and hot milk' with a fruit that turned into worms when eaten; if anyone were to sleep under its shade 'their head swells and they grow blind'. The leaves of the tree contain an irritant.

The Reach Falls, near Manchioneal, are among the most spectacular in the island. Turn off the main road just before the Driver's River Bridge and proceed with caution – for the road is rough – for two miles to a fork in the road, where an unobtrusive sign points down some steps to the falls and caves. Without doubt the falls will be 'developed' as an attraction but, as they now are, they have an unspoiled charm.

Continue through Manchioneal and along the Ken Jones Highway, named after a young Jamaican legislator who was born at Hectors River and died tragically. At Hectors River (50 miles) there is a Quaker's Chapel and an excellent secondary school, Happy Grove, which was founded early in the century by American Quakers.

The road leads on to Quao Hill, named after a Maroon Chief; from the summit there is a view of Holland Point, the island's most easterly tip, and of part of a wide fertile plain watered by the Plaintain Garden River. Descend the escarpment, and drive through Hordley to Golden Grove, in the middle of the Holland Estate. The mountains recede and the ribbon of coastal plain broadens out into fields of sugar-cane, coconuts, bananas and pastures for cattle. Though now the south coast, it is not beyond the rain-bearing influence of the trade winds. There is also a change from the small-holder economy and culture of the Blue Mountain valleys to the estate economy based, originally, on sugar.

Holland Estate once belonged to Simon Taylor, who sat in the Jamaica House of Assembly from 1763 to 1810. The richest West Indian planter of his time, he boasted that on his death his nephew Simon would be the richest commoner in England. He hated the Baptist and Methodist missionaries who preached against slavery, insisting that slaves should be treated as human beings. He had a fierce reputation for detesting women, but he fathered a number of children on his various estates.

Lady Nugent, in her diary, tells of the vast meals with which Simon Taylor entertained her husband Governor Nugent and herself. On parting, he said, 'I am very sorry, Ma'am, but good Almighty God, I must go home and cool coppers.' She thought he was referring to some sugar-making process but 'I found he meant he must go home and be abstemious, after so much feasting'. Continue to Bath, 37 miles further on, in Lady Nugent's day 'truly a lovely village at the bottom of an immense mountain'.

160

The Bath Botanical Gardens and the Bath Spa

In the second half of the eighteenth century the British and French governments recognised the importance of augmenting the food-supply in their Caribbean sugar colonies by introducing new forms of starch. Cook's voyages in the Pacific had also stimulated an interest in botany. Botanical gardens were founded in a number of West Indian islands, such as St Vincent, Dominica and Jamaica. The Bath Gardens are full of a variety of plants, breadfruit, cabbage trees, jack-fruit, cinnamon, the star apple, whose leaf is bronze on one side, bright green on the other side, and the otaheite tree which has a bright pink blossom, like a tassel.

The Bath Spa is two miles beyond the town. Lady Nugent, modestly clad in night-cap, dressing gown and pokey bonnet, set off on horseback along the narrow winding path to the spa, which contained four rooms, with a marble bath in each.

Then there is another house for infirm negroes . . . they tell you of wonderful cures performed by the waters . . . which I really found most delightful and refreshing.

The old woman attending the bath was very anxious to see her but her pokey bonnet covered her face and her dressing-gown concealed her person.

Stepping out of the bath in a perfectly undisguised state, she heard a voice near her and perceived, under the door, a pair of black eyes, and indeed a whole black face, looking earnestly at her; for the door was half-a-yard too short . . . and [the old woman] laid herself down on her stomach to peep . . . The Governor's Lady let out a great squall and away ran the old lady.

The Bath was opened in 1699, after a slave told how the water had cured his ulcerated leg. The Government bought 1300 acres of land around the spring; or perhaps 'springs' would be more accurate since hot radioactive springs and cooler water pour out of the same igneous rocks above Sulphur River. The water is mixed in the Baths to a comfortable bathing temperature. It contains lime and sulphur as well as other minerals, and is of great benefit to persons suffering from skin troubles of various sorts, and from various rheumatic ailments.

Driving west toward Kingston, the names Morant and Yallahs testify to the period of Spanish settlement when cattle were let loose on the *hato* of Morante and around the salt ponds at Yallahs. The highway by-passes Morant Bay, chief town of the parish of St Thomas, but it would be a pity not to drive through and to stop however briefly at the Court House to look at the memorial to Paul Bogle, which was created by Jamaica's leading sculptor, Edna Manley.

Morant Bay and St Thomas are of special interest to all Jamaicans because of the rising which took place here in 1865, when discontent bred by three years of drought, repressive and unjust laws and an authoritarian Governor, provoked an outbreak. Paul Bogle led a demonstration of peasants from his church in Stony Gut to

Paul Bogle statue
[MARTIN MORDECAI]

Morant Bay. Rioting broke out, the Court House was burnt down and the Custos was killed along with a number of white planters who were in the Court House. Disturbances broke out in other parts of the parish. The Governor, Eyre, called out the troops and the rising was put down with great cruelty, four hundred and fifty people being executed, six hundred flogged and more than a thousand buildings destroyed. Paul Bogle was hanged. George William Gordon was taken from Kingston to Morant Bay and hanged. The Governor considered that Gordon had fomented the rebellion because he had championed the cause of the peasants and was a friend of Bogle's. The statue to Bogle stands in front of the Court House. Behind it, looking out to the harbour, is a memorial to those who died for their part in the rising.

The Morant Bay rising marked a turning point in Jamaica's history, because it resulted in the surrender by the House of Assembly of the old representative system of government and in the institution of Crown Colony rule. St Thomas influenced the island's cultural development because it became the home, after the emancipation of the slaves in 1833, of a number of free Africans who were imported as contract workers. They brought with them their *cumina* cult and dances, and these fed strength into indigenous art forms. From earlier plantation times the legend of Three-Finger Jack was preserved. He was a black Robin Hood, who frequented the lonely hills around Bull Bay and White Horse, robbing and plundering, but never molesting the poor.

Leaving Morant Bay for Kingston, pass over the Bustamante Bridge, one of the longest in Jamaica, and continue by way of Rozelle, a pleasant picnic spot, Yallahs, Grants Pen and Bull Bay. The arid fields and eroded hills are in sharp contrast to the green cane-fields and luxuriant foliage of eastern St Thomas. You have passed into the shadow of the mountains, which bar the rain-bearing north-east trade winds.

| 13 |

Kingston, Port Royal, Spanish Town and the Blue Mountains

General information

Could one design a more perfect stage-setting, one richer in theatre, in drama?

In the background is the Blue Mountain range, reaching up to the sky. In the dawn, the highest peaks are set afire by the rising sun, and at evening they are soft lilac. In the middle distance are the Port Royal mountains, with vertical valleys like the sculptured folds of Greek sculpture; and land that slides gently from six hundred feet to sea-level. In the foreground there are twenty-five square miles of water almost encircled by a thin protecting strip of land. At dawn the enclosed water is pigeon grey and the outer sea restless celadon green.

Kingston grew out of the ashes of disaster. Today it is the capital of Jamaica, the island's chief commercial centre, and the largest city in the Commonwealth Caribbean. Its buildings cover an area of more than twenty-five square miles and its suburbs climb up Long Mountain, Jacks Hill, Stony Hill and the Red Hills. In 1690 none of this existed. At the harbour's edge there were some fishermen's huts. The great centre of trade was Port Royal, across the harbour. The island's capital was Spanish Town, which had been founded by the Spanish colonists. In 1692 an earthquake destroyed Port Royal, and some merchants moved to Kingston. They lived there in huts made with boughs, while others remained in Port Royal and attempted to make a fresh start. Two or three fires frustrated their efforts, and they also moved across the harbour.

The names of some of the city streets go back to this early period. Port Royal Street reminds us of the Port Royal merchants to whom land was allotted on the waterfront. Barry Street is named after Colonel Samuel Barry, who first owned the land; Beeston Street is named after William Beeston, Governor of the island at the end of the century, who bought the land from Barry. North, East and West Streets mark the limits of the old city, which was in the shape of a grid-iron, with an open space in the centre, the Parade, now the Parade Gardens.

Port Royal, commanding the entrance to the harbour, grew in importance as a naval base, while Kingston became by 1703 the island's chief port of entry and commercial centre. In 1872 the seat of government was moved from Spanish Town to Kingston.

In 1907 the city, which had survived a number of fires and hurricanes, was severely damaged by an earthquake and by fire. The city was rebuilt and expanded rapidly, outgrowing its old system of administration based on a small municipality; so in 1923 parts of the parish of St Andrew were merged with Kingston to form the Corporation of Kingston and St Andrew, administered by a Mayor and Corporation.

Commercial Kingston also outgrew its former limits, and New Kingston was developed to accommodate hotels, banks, commercial offices and a shopping plaza. An industrial estate was laid out in west Kingston, and a modern deep-water harbour was created at Newport West, with a free port and facilities for transhipment. Low and middle income housing estates were built, and satellite towns were established, such as Havendale and Independence City.

The Kingston waterfront has been transformed. A foreshore road spans Hunts Bay and brings Port Henderson within ten minutes of Kingston. There are ghettos and squalid slums in parts of west and eastern Kingston, but impressive progress has been made in creating a capital city worthy of its incomparable setting. For an up-to-date list of Kingston hotels, restaurants and guest houses, please apply to the Jamaica Tourist Board, 21 Dominica Drive, Kingston 5.

Places of interest

Downtown   The Institute of Jamaica; The Bank of Jamaica's Coin and Note Museum; Kingston Parish Church; Craft Market; Headquarters House and Gordon House; Heroes Park; The National Gallery of Jamaica; The Cultural Centre.

Kingston waterfront *overleaf* [MARTIN MORDECAI]

Midtown and New Kingston   Devon House
Mona   The Hope Botanical Gardens; the University of the West Indies.

Downtown

The Institute of Jamaica, 12 East Street, Kingston. This is a treasure house, near the waterfront, with a Natural History Museum, History Gallery, and a National Library, formerly the West India Reference Library. Founded in 1879 'for the encouragement of literature, science and art', it houses Jamaica's great cultural heritage, with a remarkable collection of maps, prints, documents and books relating to Jamaica and the West Indies. Its herbarium contains many specimens of Jamaican and West Indian plants, with a first-class section of Jamaican ferns; and it has a comprehensive collection of Jamaican butterflies as well as of other insects. Cultural activities include exhibitions of work by Jamaican artists.

The building stands on the site of a popular boarding house, Date Tree Hall, of the 1850s. This is associated with the name of Mary Seacole, whose portrait hangs in the gallery. She gained a great reputation as a nurse in a terrible cholera epidemic of 1850 in Jamaica; later, in Central America, she was known as 'the yellow woman from Jamaica with the cholera medicine'. In 1854, after the Crimean war between Britain, France, Turkey and Russia broke out, Mary Seacole made her way to the Crimea, met Florence Nightingale, established herself in a rough wooden building near Balaclava which she called the British Hotel, and got on with the job of nursing and feeding the soldiers who called her 'Mother Seacole'. Queen Victoria decorated her with two medals for her services to the troops. There is on display in the Museum a small terracotta bust of her by Count Gleichen, a nephew of Queen Victoria.

The 'Shark Papers' are among the Institute's most famous exhibits. In 1799, while Britain and France were at war, a British frigate, HMS *Sparrow,* patrolling off the coast of Haiti, sighted a brig with a damaged mast, boarded her and sent her as a prize of war to Port Royal, for trial in the Court of Vice-Admiralty. The German owners of the brig, the *Nancy*, and the master contested the case and produced papers that seemed satisfactory. The *Sparrow*, under Commander Wylie, continued its patrol off the south coast of Haiti, in company with a small tender, the *Ferret*, commanded by

Lieutenant Fitton. Some sailors on the *Ferret* caught a shark, pulled it aboard, cut it up, and found in its stomach a bundle of papers. Soon afterwards Wylie, in conversation with Fitton, referred to the trial of the *Nancy* and Fitton said, 'I have her papers'. 'But,' replied Wylie, 'I sealed up those papers and sent them in with her.' 'Those were the false papers,' replied Fitton. 'Here are the real ones.' The shark papers and some found in the captain's cabin in a case of salt meat proved the case against the *Nancy*, which was condemned as a prize of war.

Kingston Crafts Market, at the west end of Harbour Street, consists of a large number of stalls, each individually owned, with displays of carvings, straw goods, pottery, beautifully embroidered cloths, and colourful ceramic figurines of considerable merit.

Kingston Parish Church, at the corner of King Street and South Parade, contains some monuments and tombstones of historic interest, such as the black marble gravestone of Admiral John Benbow, who attacked a French squadron off Cartagena in 1702, and was deserted by two of his captains who were later court-martialled and shot. Benbow had his leg shattered by chain-shot, but he continued to direct the action. He was brought back to Port Royal where he died of his wounds. In the north transept there is a monument to a goldsmith, John Wolmer, whose bequest made possible the founding of Wolmer's School in 1736.

Headquarters House and Gordon House are on Duke Street, across the road from each other. Jamaica's Parliament meets at Gordon House, named in honour of George William Gordon. Of greater interest architecturally is Headquarters House, built about the middle of the eighteenth century by Thomas Hibbert, a Kingston merchant. The story goes that four rich Kingston merchants made a wager as to who could build the finest mansion, and that Hibbert won.

Heroes Park Continue north up Duke Street, cross over North Street, which marked the northern limits of the old city, to Heroes Park, which occupies the southern part of the old Kingston Race Course. The Park contains monuments to the builders of modern Jamaica; George William Gordon and Paul Bogle who were executed for their part in the Morant Bay rising, Marcus Garvey, William Alexander Bustamante and Norman Washington Manley.

Further north are two of the oldest educational institutions in Jamaica. Wolmer's School was founded in 1736 through a bequest from a Kingston jeweller, John Wolmer; this was just eighteen years after Elihu Yale's benefaction led to the founding of Yale University.

To the north of Wolmer's is Mico College. The story of its founding begins in 1670, when Barbary pirates were terrorising the Mediterranean, and taking Christians as slaves. In 1670 Lady Mico left £1000 'for the redemption of poor Christian slaves in Barbary'. When there were no longer Christian slaves in Barbary, the pirates having been eliminated by Admiral Blake, the money accumulated, reaching £120 000 in 1827. Sir Thomas Fowell Buxton, a friend of Wilberforce and a keen emancipator, prepared a programme, which the British Court of Chancery accepted, for using the money to promote education among the black and coloured population of British Guyana and the West Indies. Mico College was founded in 1838 with money from the Mico Trust. Since then it has trained teachers for service in the elementary schools of Jamaica, as well as for some of the other islands. Its alumni have a distinguished record of public service and of educational work at every level in the island. It is not too much to say that old Miconians and the alumni of the various teacher-training colleges for women, St Josephs, Bethlehem and Shortwood, were among the foremost in providing Jamaica with the trained minds, the idealism and the loyalty that independence demands.

Midtown

Devon House is highly recommended. It was built in 1881 by a Jamaican architect. It passed through other hands and, by the gift of another merchant, Percy Lindo, is now the property of the Government of Jamaica. Recently redecorated, it is now one of the finest cultural centres in Jamaica, elegantly furnished, with shops that display some of the island's finest work in jewellery, fabrics,

Devon House *opposite* [JAMAICA TOURIST BOARD, NEW YORK]

carvings and straw work. It also has a grog shop, a coffee shop and gourmet restaurant and is altogether a delightfully refreshing place.

Mona

The Royal Botanical Gardens at Hope cover 150 acres of the north-east corner of the Liguanea Plain, at the foot of the hills, on part of what used to be the Hope Sugar Estate. Some of the aqueducts survive here and on the grounds of the nearby University of the West Indies. The setting is magnificent: spacious lawns, ornamental gardens and borders of bougainvillaea of many varieties which are ablaze with yellows, purples, reds and whites early in the year, against a background of hills with loftier peaks in the distance. There is a highly prized collection of more than two hundred species of orchids. The people of Kingston frequent the gardens on holidays and at weekends, special attractions being a children's garden, called Coconut Park, a maze and a small zoo, with lions and tigers, monkeys, snakes and crocodiles.

The University of the West Indies, founded in 1948, occupies a square mile of land on the Mona Common, once the Hope Sugar Estate; a brick aqueduct survives, which took water from the Hope River to the fields of the estate. The Chapel was built from the stones of a ruined Georgian building on a Trelawny sugar estate, Gayle's Valley. The Master Builders of Jamaica took down the old building and transported the stones to Kingston where the University's architects, Norman and Dawbarn, through their local representative Alick Low, designed the new building and supervised its erection.

The University started with thirty-two students. It is supported by fourteen countries of the Commonwealth Caribbean. It now has an enrolment of some 15 000 graduate and undergraduate students, with a campus at St Augustine in Trinidad, another at Cave Hill in Barbados, and offices and programmes in all the other supporting countries. It reflects the essential unity of the widely-dispersed West Indian nations. Like the University of the South West Pacific, its campus includes a vast expanse of sea.

The University has Schools of Medicine, Agriculture, Management, Engineering and Law, as well as of the Humanities and the Natural and Social Sciences. It has a region-wide extension programme.

**Main administrative complex of the Mona Campus
of the University of the West Indies**
[UNIVERSITY OF THE WEST INDIES]

Port Royal is situated at the end of the Palisades, a natural break-water seven miles long. The English fortified the point in the 1660s so as to command the entrance to the harbour and, within a few years, many English buccaneers had made this their base for raids against Spanish America. The city grew rapidly, and became notorious for its wickedness: it was the Babylon of the West, a City of Gold, The Wickedest Place in Christendom, a Gilded Hades where common seamen hung their ears with heavy gold rings studded with gems, where dagger thrusts were as common as brawls, and the body of a murdered man would remain in a dance-room until the dancing was over. The taverns rang with the exploits of Henry Morgan, who took and sacked Porto Bello, and brought back 300 000 pieces of eight; then 250 000 pieces of eight from burning Maracaibo; and 750 000 pieces from Panama on the Pacific Coast. Made Governor of Jamaica in 1682, and ordered by the King to put an end to the attacks on Spain and to buccaneering, Morgan offered his former companions a choice between a grant of land and the end of a rope. His way of life made him an old man at forty-five, 'his eyes yellowish, his belly jutting out a little'. With death near, he turned from his doctors to an African medicine man who poulticed him with urine and plastered him over with clay. This finished him off. He died in 1688.

Four years later, while the Rector of the Parish Church was taking a glass of wormwood with the acting Governor, the earth heaved and shook. 'Be not afeard,' the Governor said, 'it will soon be over.' Within three minutes Port Royal was destroyed. The frigate *Swan* in the careening yard keeled over on to one side, the land sank with quays and warehouses, and a tidal wave swept the *Swan* inland, riding high above the roofs. Running towards Morgans Fort, the Rector saw the earth open and swallow a number of people. He hurried past men and women buried up to their necks, some upside down. A tombstone, now in the yard of the Parish Church, records how a French refugee, Lewis Galdey, was swallowed up in the great earthquake . . . 'and by the Providence of God was by another Shock Thrown into the sea . . .'

John Pike, a Quaker who survived the earthquake, wrote to his brother saying:

'I lost my wife, my son, a 'prentice, a white maid and six slaves . . . My land . . . is all sunk; a good sloop may sail over it as well as over the Point.' The wretched survivors left without shelter, regarded *'a house that is daubed with mortar and thatched, the eaves hanging down almost to the ground, a pleasant house . . . Here you may see colonels and great men bowing down their bodies to creep into a little hutch.'*

Port Royal remained important as a naval base, however, with ships of the line swinging at anchor off the Dockyard. Horatio Nelson, then a frail-looking young officer, kept watch from his quarterdeck on Fort Charles. A year later he was brought back from a sortie against Nicaragua, near death from yellow fever and dysentery. A black woman, Cuba Cornwallis, nursed him back to health. Cuba, who had been a slave, had been freed by Admiral Cornwallis, whose name she took. Over the entrance to Fort Charles are the arms of Nelson. The wall bears this inscription: 'In this place dwelt Horatio Nelson. You who tread his footprints remember his glory.'

Along with **Fort Charles** other places of special interest are **St Peter's Church**, where memorial tablets on the wall record the deaths of young midshipmen from yellow fever, cholera and dysentery. The silver plate of the Church is said to have been part

Port Royal [JAMAICA JOURNAL]

of the booty Morgan brought back from Panama. Near to the Fort stands the old Naval Hospital, now an Archaeological Museum, with artefacts from the submerged part of the city. The pioneer in this effort at recreating Port Royal's past was an American, Edward Link, who in 1959 located the sunken walls of houses, and recovered cannon-barrels and domestic items including a brass watch dated 1686 whose hands had stopped at 11:43, the time of the earthquake. The hands had disappeared but X-ray pictures revealed traces of them.

The University of the West Indies maintains a **Marine Biology Research Station at Port Royal**. Visitors interested in learning about the research and teaching programmes should make contact with the Public Relations officer of the University, (Tel: (809)-927-9925).

Morgan's Harbour Hotel, Beach Club and Marina, (Tel: (809)-938-7223), on the eastern side of Port Royal, can be reached by ferry from Ocean Boulevard, Kingston, or by car or taxi from the Norman Manley International Airport or from Kingston by way

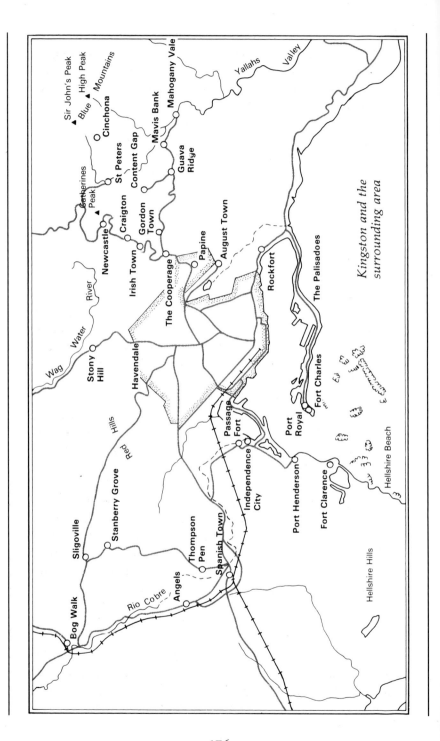

Kingston and the surrounding area

of Rockfort. The hotel has a large seafront patio, a marina with boats moored along the jetty, a restaurant and bar, and a swimming area which is roped off from the boating area. From the patio there is a view across the harbour to Kingston and the mountains. The setting is superb, the atmosphere friendly and relaxed, the management quietly efficient. There are twenty-five rooms, with showers and air-conditioning; à la carte meals; excellent sea-food. Club membership secures a discount on the rate for the rooms as well as the facility for signing accounts which can then be settled in full at the end of your stay.

Spanish Town

Capital of Jamaica's largest parish, St Catherine, with a population of 50 000, Spanish Town combines a vigorous present with a lively sense of past greatness. Dwellings, shops and factories straggle along the highway that leads to Kingston, Ocho Rios, Mandeville; squatters live in ramshackle huts within barriers of broken sheets of galvanised iron and farm pocket-handkerchief scraps of land; children and traders throng the streets, trucks move to the market with produce, cars and taxis hurry along the by-pass road with little thought of history and memorials. The people of Spanish Town, however, treasure their city's past. They know that today's animation and bustle are repeated in every Jamaican town, but that no other city in the Commonwealth Caribbean is as rich in historic buildings and records as theirs is.

The story begins in 1534 when Spanish colonists abandoned their first capital city, New Seville, a mile west of St Anns Bay, and moved to Spanish Town, which they called Villa de la Vega, The City of the Plain. As was the custom of all Spanish colonists, they planned a city around a central square, erected administrative buildings and a church, on whose foundations the present Cathedral stands, and also built a Franciscan monastery. The names of some of the city streets remind us of the church and the monks: White Church Street, Red Church Street, Monk Street, for example.

The site was well-chosen. The Rio Cobre provided water, the surrounding land was fertile, and an inland location gave some protection from pirates; not completely, however, for three English 'gentlemen adventurers' attacked it: Anthony Shirley in 1597,

Rodney Memorial [JACKIE SCOTT]

Newport in 1603, Jackson in 1640. These were damaging but temporary set-backs. Finally, in 1655 an English invading force landed at Passage Fort, by the mouth of the Rio Cobre, took the city, and made it the capital of their new colony.

For two centuries Spanish Town was Jamaica. The Governor lived there, the Supreme Court sat there, and the Council and Assembly met there to enact the laws by which the island was governed.

Lady Nugent tells of her arrival in 1805.

I was received at the entrance to Kings House by Lord Balcarres, some of the members of the Council and Assembly, and the gentlemen of his own family, all with yellow wrinkled faces . . .

Up at 6 o'clock and much amused till 8 (when we break-fasted) at seeing the black population and the odd appearance of everything from my windows. The Kings House, which is now our residence, is a large brick building of two stories high, forming one side of a square; opposite is the House of Assembly; the other two sides are formed by a Guard House and Public Buildings. Our apartments are very spacious but very dirty . . .

A handsome building, the Kings House was completed about 1762,

178

and it remained the Governor's residence up to 1872, when the capital was moved to Kingston. In 1925 much of old Kings House was destroyed by fire, the facade alone being preserved. Within the stables, which have been reconditioned, is a Folk Museum, part of a project for establishing a cultural centre at the site.

The Spaniards laid out the square, but no trace of their buildings remains. Rodney's memorial stands on the northern side of the square, alongside the island's record office; just behind is a modern building that houses the Archives, a notable collection of papers, including some that date back to the period of Washington, Jefferson and others. On the east side of the square is the House of Assembly, which is now used as a school.

The other building of greatest historical value is the Cathedral, which stands on the site of the Spanish Chapel of the Red Cross which was destroyed by the English invaders. The walls are covered with monuments, some of them by the outstanding sculptors of their day; the most notable is that to the Earl and Countess of Effingham, a work of flowing grace and beauty.

The first government archivist, Clinton Blake, has written an interesting and comprehensive guide to the City of Spanish Town. Those who plan visiting the old capital will find this little book invaluable.

Kingston-based tours

Being the island's capital, Kingston is well-served with roads and air-services. As from the hub of a wheel, highways extend east, west and to the north, providing linkages with all the resort areas. A visitor has many options: a day or more in Ocho Rios or Port Antonio, in Mandeville, Negril, Montego Bay; at Bath or the Milk River Spa; half a day in Spanish Town or Port Royal; a picnic on the Hellshire Beach; an excursion to Blue Mountain Peak; a weekend at Pine Grove in the Blue Mountain range; a tour of the coffee country around Mavis Bank; an afternoon's drive to Newcastle, 3700 feet above Kingston yet only an hour away by car; a picnic at Castleton Gardens in the valley of the Wag Water River; a tour of Spanish Town and the Bog Walk Gorge, returning by way of the Red Hills.

One's interests help one to decide. Often it is possible to combine the present with the past, by including, for example, Spanish Town with the Hellshire Beach. Nature lovers, especially gardeners and botanists, will find the Botanical Gardens of absorbing interest. The mountains minister to most of us, lifting us out of ourselves with panoramic views of the Liguanea Plains, Kingston harbour, the magnificent Yallahs Valley and the Peak.

The tour desk in the hotel, the hotel staff and any of the Jamaica Tourist Board offices or tour operators can provide information and give advice. Also, consider the options for getting around: whether to rent a car or join two or three other visitors in hiring a car or a limousine or joining a group travelling by mini-bus.

Since there are so many options it is not possible to describe each route in detail. There are, however, a few tours that have a special appeal for lovers of the sea, of gardens, of mountain country, of hiking and camping.

Hellshire Beach   Within easy reach of Kingston, Hellshire Beach offers swimming and snorkelling, with a sparkling beach. It is very popular with Kingstonians who for generations were barred from the beach by wild scrub and hostile cactus country. Those of us who lived in Kingston got into the habit of thinking that good swimming and white-sand beaches were two hours away on the north coast, when they were actually on our doorstep. There is a good route which brings together the past and present. Take the road that leads along the Kingston waterfront from Breezy Castle to the foreshore road, Marcus Garvey Drive and the Causeway to Portmore and Port Henderson. The narrow crowded lanes and old wharves of downtown Kingston have been replaced by boulevards and open spaces, so that now Kingston can enjoy its splendid waterfront. In contrast, Port Henderson speaks of the days of Nelson and Rodney. The latter had his look-out in the hills above the port. The old houses have been restored, and one can recapture the charm and graciousness of the stonework and wooden beams. Then go on to the beach. Return by way of the Caymanas Race Course and The Ferry.

Castleton Botanical Gardens   Jamaica has a priceless heritage in its botanic gardens at Bath, Cinchona, Castleton and the Hope Gardens. Three of these show the influence of the famous Kew Gardens of London, for Nathaniel Wilson and Robert Thompson, who laid them out between 1869 and 1880, were trained at Kew.

Snorkelling in the clear waters off Jamaica's coast [JAMAICA TOURIST BOARD, KINGSTON]

Each garden has its own individuality, through differences in temperature, rainfall and altitude.

The Castleton Gardens cover fifteen acres in the Wag Water Gorge, nineteen miles from Kingston on the Junction Road. At Hope the average annual rainfall is forty-five inches; at Castleton it is a hundred and fifteen inches, so *ixora*, azaleas and *dracaena* flourish. Flowering trees fill the place with colour throughout most of the year. Tree ferns, a lily pond, many varieties of palms, towering graceful trees, lawns and the sound of the river combine to make this a place of quiet beauty. The guide who takes you around is sure to show you one of the curiosities of the garden, the trap door spider.

On the return trip it is worth taking one of the side roads that branch off from the A3 at Stony Hill; either the Old Stony Hill road on the right, or the road on the left that runs along one of the mountain ridges overlooking Kingston. From either of these there are extensive views of the Liguanea Plain and Kingston Harbour.

The Blue Mountains

Pine Grove, owned and run by Ronnie and Marcia Thwaites, is the best base from which to explore the old coffee country of Jamaica, to visit the garden at Cinchona, to climb Blue Mountain Peak. Leave Kingston by the Hope Road or Old Hope Road, and continue beyond Papine by a road that runs alongside the Hope River to Gordon Town. The first famous botanical garden of Jamaica was established nearby at Spring Garden by Hinton East. This supplied the island with a variety of plants and fruit trees that were imported during the last quarter of the eighteenth century.

At Gordon Town, by the police station, take the road that branches right to Guava Ridge and Mavis Bank. Guava Ridge is the home of one of Jamaica's most highly acclaimed products, the Old Jamaica Liqueurs, produced and bottled by Ian Sangster, a Scotsman who built his factory at World's End, made Jamaica his home, and provided her with a valuable resource. Mr Sangster invites visitors to tour the factory which is on five levels, to sample the liqueurs and to enjoy the view of Newcastle from the terrace.

Pine Grove Hotel is near the junction at the bus station beyond World's End. The main road leads on to Mavis Bank. The road that branches left climbs up to the hotel, which has a number of chalets equipped with facilities for self-catering. The atmosphere is informal and helpful without ever being intrusive.

Those who wish to see the old coffee country of Jamaica and to visit Cinchona should follow a route leading to Valda, Content Gap and Clydesdale, formerly a coffee plantation, now a forestry station. The plant was introduced into the island in 1728, but the industry did not develop until the last quarter of that century, when Britain reduced its excise duties on coffee and the Haitian revolution practically destroyed that country's export trade. A mile or so from Content Gap there is one of the best known of the coffee Great Houses of that period, Charlottenberg.

Cinchona is four miles from Clydesdale. Those who take the stiff uphill walk to the Gardens, or who choose to follow the rough road by way of Westphalia, will find an ample reward awaiting them.

The gardens are named after the cinchona tree, the bark of which was a source of quinine. The tree was introduced from Peru by Nathaniel Wilson and plants were supplied to private owners for cultivation, the Government providing them with large tracts of mountain land on easy terms. At first the project made money, but

The Blue Mountains (Granville Allen)
[JAMAICA TOURIST BOARD, KINGSTON]

the price of the bark fell and exportation came to an end.

The late Aimee Webster, in her book *Caribbean Gardening*, gives a vivid picture of the gardens.

Snow in a tropical garden! So seem the frosts of white alyssum that edge formal beds of white narcissi at Cinchona. A scene of bold white and green is the great lawn bordered by white roses and white azaleas along white gravel walks ... Spice laden pinks, the mingled odours of violet, nicotiana, honeysuckle pervade Cinchona Gardens. In wooded sections the aromas of camphor, cinnamon and pine are pungent. Beneath magnolia and rhododendron in March until early June blue agapanthus and pink belladonna stand ... Heliotrope and hydrangea grow profusely ... Cowslips and field daisies are wild. Bright as new copper pennies are Australian poppies ... Despite the glory of colour, the immediate impression is one of countless tones of green: green of bracken, silky oak, cork, fir ...

From the gardens it is possible to pick out St Johns Peak to the north, and the main range of the Blue Mountains from the garden's Panoramic Walk.

183

Hiking in the Blue Mountains
[JAMAICA TOURIST BOARD, KINGSTON]

There is evidence of an expanding coffee industry. This was spear-headed by pioneers such as Keble Munn, who has his coffee factory at Mavis Bank, and by the Government of Jamaica. The number of coffee planters has increased, many of them being smallholders who cultivate the coffee and then take it to be processed at a central factory. Notable too is the development which is being undertaken by the Japanese. In 1981 they bought Craigton Great House near Irish Town and they are pushing ahead energetically with extensive plantings of coffee on the northern slopes beyond Hardwar Gap.

So many places deserve a visit that it is not possible to name them all. Hikers and nature lovers are advised to make contact with the Government of Jamaica's Forestry Department for information about camping sites and forest reserves. For example, those visiting Newcastle can include the Hollywell Natural Forest, on the slopes around Hardwar Gap. The Forestry Department has a two-bedroom house at Clydesdale which can be leased, but the tenant must provide for himself.

The Peak

The trip is not difficult, provided it is carefully planned beforehand.

The Pine Grove Hotel is a good base from which to start. Proceed to Guava Ridge, and take the Mavis Bank road which leads down through pinewoods to the Falls River and Mavis Bank. Munn's Mavis Bank Central Coffee Factory processes the coffee brought in by more than 3000 smallholders. Visitors are welcome.

Proceed from Mavis Bank to Mahogany Vale and Hagley Gap, and by a rough dirt road on the left to Fern Hill, then to Whitfield Hall, the last dwelling house on the way up to the Peak. Hikers usually overnight here, and then set off early in the morning on a three-hour walk up a steep track, making their way through mist and through elfin woodland which starts at about 5000 feet, and through scrub to a dome rather than a peak.

> ... *a little baldish flat of grass scrubbed with bilberry and blackberry bushes* ...
> *If the dawn were clear* ... *the innocence of daybreak revealed the island like a cut beryl set in a glassy sea. The sharp ranges were of precious stone. The rivers lay veiled like opal serpents. Port Antonio shone in the ring of its harbor* ... *far away to the north-east the thin pale line of Cuba was steady against the pale blue of sea and sky.*

But try for a clear dawn. Kenneth Pringle, from whom I have quoted, says he only had four fine days out of a fortnight. The locals can best advise on what preparation to make and what months are best for making the trip. Here are two useful addresses:

The Jamaica Government Forests Department,
173 Constant Spring Road,
Kingston 10
Tel: (809)-924-2612/2626

The Jamaica Camping and Hiking Association,
PO Box 216,
Kingston 7
Tel: (809)-927-5409.

The office is at the top of Jacks Hill, four miles up the Jacks Hill Road from the Barbican area; five minutes by car. There is a bus service.

| 14 |
Explore a region – the South Coast, Mandeville and Milk River Spa

General information

It's more than an area – it's a region as large as Curaçao or Aruba, extending along the south coast for eighty miles from Milk River and Calabash Bay through Alligator pond to Savanna-la-Mar, capital of Westmoreland. It reaches inland to include two places of special interest, Mandeville, twenty miles north of Alligator Pond, and the Milk River Spa, six miles inland from the mouth of the Milk River, and fifty miles from Kingston. The key points are Mandeville, the Milk River Spa, Treasure Beach near Alligator Pond, and Bluefields to the west.

Visitors are just discovering the South Coast, especially those in search of a natural holiday, a vacation with the family on quiet beaches, a health vacation, a fishing and snorkelling holiday.

The first impression is of space, because the coastal plain is wider than on the north coast; but the physical configuration is the same, so that you can climb from the plain up a series of escarpments to green inland terraces and plateaux. At some points the ridge ends abruptly at the shore, as at Lover's Leap which stands 1600 feet above the sea. At Swamp there is a fantasy-land of lagoons; at Lacovia a two-mile long bamboo avenue; and from the top of Spur Tree Hill a view of the Westmoreland Plain.

We sample the country and its history first in our tour from Negril by way of Sav-la-Mar to Mandeville. Then, after establishing a base there we make two tours, one to the Milk River Spa and some old plantations rich in historic interest, the other right across central Jamaica from Mandeville to the north coast, to Discovery Bay and Ocho Rios.

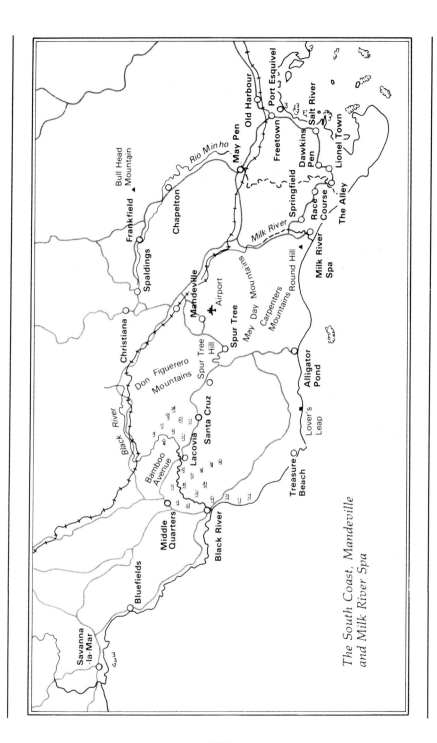

*The South Coast, Mandeville
and Milk River Spa*

The South Coast – Negril to Mandeville

**Negril – Retreat – Little London – Savanna-la-Mar –
Ferris Cross – Sav-la-Mar – Whitehouse – Bluefields –
Black River – Santa Cruz – Spur Tree Hill – Mandeville**
The route reminds us that Jamaica is several Caribbean islands in
one. Negril borders Hanover, one of Jamaica's most mountainous
parishes with the physical contours and much of the charm of
Grenada. In contrast, Westmoreland, with its luxuriant cane-fields,
bamboos, spreading pastures, cattle, and its vivid reminders of India
as well as of Africa, bring the Caroni plains of Trinidad to mind.
Then, gradually, after leaving Black River, we move from the coastal
plain and climb the limestone escarpment to the pastures and limestone crags of Jamaica's gracious uplands, in parts so much like the
larger uplands of the Dominican Republic.

Encounter with yesterday

To drive from Negril by way of Retreat and Little London is to
encounter the eighteenth and nineteenth centuries, to hear again
creaking carts laden with hogsheads of sugar, to see old sugar works
become bustling centres of estates such as those at Fort William and
Roaring River, and to catch whispers of old scandals and romances.
The visitor can capture much of Jamaica's past as a sugar and coffee
island by purchasing Professor Barry Higman's splendid *Jamaica
Surveyed*, which describes with a wealth of detail eighteenth and
nineteenth century Jamaica plantation maps and plans.

Higman reminds us of one of the many links between the North
American colonies and Jamaica. Two Westmoreland Estates –
Friendship and Greenwich – belonged to wealthy Robert Vassall
whose family came to Jamaica from Massachusetts in the 1670s. His
daughter, Elizabeth Vassall, was born at Sweet River Pen near the
estates, in 1770. She went to England as a young girl, married Sir
Geoffrey Webster at an early age, fell in love with Henry Richard,
3rd Baron Holland, was divorced on the grounds of adultery,
married the Earl in 1797, and soon became one of the most
celebrated hostesses of the period. With her husband she made
Holland House in London the meeting-place of 'a brilliant circle of
statesmen, wits, and men of letters which gave the house a European
celebrity' (Higman).

Another Westmoreland sugar planter who was a welcome guest at Holland House was Matthew Gregory Lewis, called 'Monk Lewis', who leapt into fame with his first novel *The Monk*, and sustained his reputation as a writer with his *Journal of a West Indian Sugar Planter* that told of visits in 1815 – 17 to his estate at Cornwall, which adjoined Friendship. Monk Lewis was disliked by many other sugar planters because they said 'he spoiled his slaves'. 'Spoiling' meant treating them like human beings, improving the estate hospital, abolishing flogging, and increasing the number of holidays. Lewis was not merely a 'do-gooder'. He deliberately adopted a humanitarian line to satisfy his own compassionate and sensitive nature.

Another neighbour of distinction was William Beekford, born in Jamaica in 1740, owner of Fort William and Williamsfield estates. Beekford left a vivid description of the devastation of Savanna-la-Mar in 1780 by a hurricane:

> *the sea drove with progressive violence for more than a mile into the country; and carried terror as it left destruction wherever it passed. Two large ships and a schooner were at anchor in the bay but were driven a considerable distance from the shore and totally wrecked among the mango trees upon the land.*

Beekford's protegée, George Robertson, the landscape artist, in the course of a visit to Jamaica, produced a number of engravings, among them two charming drawings of the estate buildings at Fort William and Roaring River (Westmoreland).

Little London   10 miles east of Negril, brings us face to face with India. The story of the East Indian members of the Jamaican community begins on a morning in 1838 when the ship *Hesperus* moved slowly up the Demerara river in Guyana and landed 156 East Indians, men and women, who left their homes in India to work on the Guyana sugar estates. A few weeks later another group arrived, and before many years had passed, the trickle of contract-workers from India had grown into a stream which flowed for 80 years.

By then there were nearly half a million East Indians in the West Indies. Most of them, 89 out of every 100, went to Guyana and Trinidad; eight out of every 100 to Jamaica, and three out of every 100 to Grenada, St Lucia, St Vincent, and Dominica. Many of those who came made their homes in the islands, enriching them with their culture and skills; and in Trinidad their settlement meant 'the emergence for the first time in the history of Trinidad of a class of small farmers' (Dr Eric Williams). The rice-fields of Westmoreland are but one illustration of the benefits Jamaica gained from their coming. Through these rice-fields flows the **Cabarita River** which is navigable for about six miles from its mouth. Alligators were once plentiful, but now they are rarely seen.

Sav-La-Mar stands near the site of **Oristan**, one of the three cities founded by early Spanish colonists. Its site has not been identified. The perils of travel in the days of wind-power, the extraordinary persistence of travellers, and the slow pace of life, are revealed by the story of a Spanish nobleman, Serrano, a passenger on one of the treasure fleets in the reign of Charles V of Spain. He was ship-wrecked near Oristan, saved himself alone and lived there in a solitary and lone condition for three years; he was then joined by another lone survivor from another shipwreck. After another four years he finally reached Spain, was sent to Germany to tell his story to the Emperor and had his reward when Charles gave him an order on the mines of Peru for 4800 ducats. Alas, Serrano died on his way to Panama to collect his money.

Bluefields, east of Sav-la-Mar, may have been named after a buccaneer, Blauvelt, who made use of the little harbour; or it may have been named after Bluefields in Nicaragua. Certainly the bay was much used as a gathering place for convoys, owing to its good anchorage.

In the days before Morse and Marconi, (comment Philip Wright and Paul White in *Exploring Jamaica*) *there was no nonsense about war-time secrecy and a typical notice in the* Jamaica Mercury *dated April 16, 1779, and signed by Admiral Peter Parker announced "Notice is hereby given a convoy will be appointed to sail from the respective parts of the island are to assemble at Bluefields and are to go through the Gulph of Florida. The men of war which are to compose the convoy*

*will sail from Port Royal the 28th day of May, and from
Bluefields the 1st day of June".*

An altogether lovely place, Bluefields' best remembered resident –
though only for eighteen months – was the celebrated English
naturalist, Philip Gosse, author of *A Naturalist's Sojourn in
Jamaica.* With great ease and sympathy he described the birds,
insects, plants and way of life at Bluefields. He stayed as paying guest
with a Moravian minister and his wife and sent back to England
specimens of insects, shells, birds, orchids. He was fortunate in the
help and friendship of one of the outstanding Jamaicans of that time,
Richard Hill. How Gosse enjoyed the unspoiled woods, and little
Bluefields River, 'a romantic little stream' teeming with mullet, crayfish and crabs, and with what regret he noted the condition of the
plantations,

> *beautiful sugar-estates . . . half desolate, and the planters had
> either ceased to reside in their mansions or had pitifully
> retrenched their expenses.*

Surinam Quarters is the name given to the area through which
we travel on our way from Bluefields to Whitehouse. The name
brings to mind one of the most fantastic deals ever made in real
estate. In 1665 the English, who had taken Surinam, a valuable sugar-
producing colony next door to Guyana, handed it back to the Dutch
who, in exchange, gave New York (then New Amsterdam) to the
English. The English resettled their Surinam planters – and their
slaves – in these parts. They were skilled in sugar production and
their arrival helped to establish sugar production in Jamaica, then
an empty island over-dependent on buccaneering.

Years later, another group of refugees settled in Surinam Quarters.
They were amongst the thousands who invested in the highly specu-
lative South Sea Company of the 1780s, and went out as settlers
to Darien. The Company collapsed. Fortunes accumulated over years
were lost in a day. The colonists were in distress. Some, mostly
Scots, were brought to Jamaica and settled in Surinam Quarters. To
these, and to other Scotch settlers, many of them Campbells in this
part of Jamaica, we owe such nostalgic Scottish names as Culloden,
Kilmarnock, Auchindown.

Whitehouse, 17½ miles from Sav-la-Mar, is widely known as a

Black River Safari tour
[JAMAICA TOURIST BOARD, KINGSTON]

fishing centre, like its satellite villages, Blue Water and Scotts Cove. There are excellent fishing banks some twelve miles or so off the coast where white marlin, sailfish, wahoo, barracuda, king fish, tuna, oceanic bonito, mackerel and snapper have been taken. The odds are that Whitehouse will become increasingly popular as visitors discover the charms of the South Coast and its potential for water-sports, fishing and crafts. Near Whitehouse there are growths of thatch palm from which generations of straw-weavers have made some of Jamaica's finest straw-work.

Black River (27.8 miles), the capital of St Elizabeth, stands at the mouth of Jamaica's largest and longest river. For years it flourished as a centre for the trade in logwood, whose dye was in high demand in Europe for dyeing textiles. When analine dyes came on the market the demand for logwood fell, and old trading centres in dyewoods, such as Belize and Black River, fell on hard times.

Black River has considerable potential as a centre for a new, exciting form of tourism, for within easy reach are a network of lagoons and small lakes quite different from anything else in Jamaica and, indeed, in the West Indies. Those who are interested in learning

193

about attractions and accommodation should contact the South Coast Management Centre or the Jamaica Tourist Board.

Lacovia, the old capital of St Elizabeth, drew its life from the Black River, for the sugar from inland estates was shipped down the river. Today, it is best known for its two-mile long avenue of bamboos, and for the Lacovia Tombstone which, according to tradition, marks the burial place of two young men who killed each other in a duel. Scepticism is justified, since the marble slab that remains speaks of a 15-year old boy, Thomas Jordan Spencer. The arms on the slab are those of Spencer of Althorp. Historians have pointed out that Charles Spencer, Earl of Sunderland, married the second daughter of John Churchill, Duke of Marlborough. Their son, the second duke, is ancestor of the present duke, as well as of Winston Churchill and of Princess Diana. Some claim that the Jordan Spencer named on the tombstone may have been a member of the English Quaker family of Jordan (Jordans), a village in Buckinghamshire and a well-known Quaker Centre.

Through Santa Cruz and Goshen the road runs to Gutters at the foot of the Spur Tree Hill, and then begins a five-mile climb to the top of the escarpment where the Kaiser Bauxite Company have their

Bamboo Avenue
[JAMAICA TOURIST BOARD, NEW YORK]

headquarters. The invaluable 'Wright' and 'White' provide the best commentary.

Spur Tree Hill is a climb of nearly five miles, with some stiff gradients and many hairpin bends. About half-way up is 'Brown Man's Cool Down', an eating-place famous for curried goat; the business has grown from a roadside stall of the 1930s where 'Brown Man's' mother handed out free coffee to the truck-drivers who stopped to cool their boiling engines. As one gets higher, majestic views unfold. Northwards runs the bastion of the Don Figueroa Mountains, and westwards the plain stretches away to the Santa Cruz massif. At the top of the hill are the Kaiser Bauxite Company Administrative Offices, 2000 feet up on the May Day mountain ridge, and looking straight down on the scarred surface of the largest open-pit mining operations in the world.

After Spur Tree the upland country opens out so that the five miles to Mandeville take us through pastureland interspersed with properties and small holdings.

Mandeville

One of Jamaica's busiest and most attractive inland towns, Mandeville, provides an excellent base from which to explore the south coast and central Jamaica. The Jamaica Tourist Board maintains an office there. It is the headquarters for the South Coast Marketing Company (SCMC) which was formed by an enterprising private sector group to promote the region as an important attractive tourist resort in its own right. The Company offers combination packages which include some, or all, of the various bases, and advises on accommodation offered by an expanding network of small hotels and villas. A choice of tours is added to each option. We look first at Mandeville, and then suggest a number of tours to various parts of the region.

Mandeville has retained its charm and relaxed character while developing into an industrial centre, the major industry being bauxite. It is the capital of the parish of Manchester, which takes its name from its creator, the Duke of Manchester. He broke all records for ceremonial longevity. He governed Jamaica for nineteen years. While he was Governor, planters and merchants who lived in outlying parts of the parishes of Westmoreland, Vere and Clarendon got together and urged the creation of a new parish, with an administrative centre within easier reach, an important consideration in an age of horse-drawn carriages. Following the example of Solomon, the Duke and the House of Assembly carved pieces out of the older parishes of St Elizabeth, Vere and Clarendon to create a new parish, which was named Manchester, after the Duke. The Duke's heir was Lord Mandeville, so the capital of the new parish was named after him.

Up to the 1950s Manchester produced cattle, pimento, citrus and vegetables. The town was the attractive social and commercial centre not only of the parish but also of a large section of central Jamaica. Being 2000 feet above sea-level it has a near-perfect climate, with a temperature rarely higher than 85°F in the summer, or lower than 55°F in the depth of winter. The night sky is brilliant with stars throughout the year, so much so that years ago two celebrated American astronomers, Hamilton and William Pickering, set up their telescopes on the edge of town.

Having secured a parish and a capital town, the Manchester people started to clamour that Mandeville, with its climate, its efficient communication network and its central location, should be made the summer capital of Jamaica. They pressed their case when Governor Sir Hugh Foot, greatly loved by all Jamaicans, visited Mandeville in the 1950s. But Hugh Foot, (the late Lord Caradon) was better versed in holy writ than were the petitioners. Resisting the pressure, he reminded them of the Biblical injunction, 'Thou shalt not suffer thy Foot to be moved.'

In the 1950s the character of this placid country town, built in 1816, with an English style village green, Parish Church and Court House and with shops and offices lining the other sides of the green, began to change. The town and its people were sitting in the centre of Jamaica's 'red earth' or bauxite country. Alcan Jamaica, one of the pioneer companies of Jamaica's bauxite industry set up its offices a mile away from the village green, and built its Kirkvine works, to process bauxite into aluminium – a pioneering effort that none of the other bauxite companies attempted at that time – five miles away, at Kendall. Modern residences and shopping centres began to spread across the pastures. Manchester and Jamaica had gained an industrial base for their economy. Some years later the Kaiser

Company set up its headquarters at Spur Tree, five miles to the south. Today, Mandeville draws its strength from agriculture and industry. The town has no ghettos. Its people are vigorous and civic-minded, representative of the townsfolk of many of the upland towns of Jamaica such as Spaldings, Christiana and Browns Town.

Restaurants

International Chinese Restaurant
117 Manchester Road, Mandeville.   Tel: 809-962-0527
Serves lunch, dinner, Cantonese style, seafood, etc.
Opening hours: 12 noon to 9:00 p.m.
Sundays by arrangement.
Caters for special occasions.

The Feeding Tree
Manchester Shopping Centre,
16 Caledonia Road, Mandeville.   Tel: 809-962-2094
Serves only lunch and dinner, open from 11:00 a.m.
Take-out service, catering service, serves only Chinese food.
Seats approximately 135 people.

Bill Laurie's Steak House
Bloomfield Gardens, Mandeville.
Lunch and dinner served, mainly Jamaican dishes.
Catering service available.
Beautiful bar.
Seats 50 inside comfortably and 200 outside.
Happy Hour Fridays – 5:30 p.m. to 6:30 p.m.; also ladies' night.
Once the Bloomfield Hotel, and now 100 years old, this one of the best restaurants in Mandeville. There is an exhibition of Bill's antiques, and a panoramic view of the town.

The Den
35 Caledonia Road, Mandeville.   Tel: 809-962-3603
Serves pizza – ham, bacon, pepperoni, salami, vegetable, cheese, lobster – as well as chicken, steak, jerked pork and chicken.
Restaurant and cocktail lounge.
Take-out service (not delivery) offered.

Stopping places

Bammy Factory
One can see how bammy is made at Mr Clement Bloomfield's home, 40 Greenvale Road, Mandeville, on Tuesdays and Wednesdays. Tel: 809-962-2821.

Cecil Charlton's Mansion
Home of Mandeville's ex-Mayor for over twenty years. The mansion, with its unusual architecture, has a beautiful garden. Visits can be arranged any day except Wednesdays and Saturdays. There is no charge but contributions to a Mandeville charity are welcome. The mansion is in Mayday district.

Dalkeith Riding Stables
Riding trails and riding lessons. Horse Shows with participation from islandwide teams are sometimes held there.

Manchester Club
Caledonia Road, Mandeville.   Tel: 809-962-2403.
Established in 1868, this members' club is the oldest in the Caribbean. It has four hard tennis courts, a nine-hole golf course, reputed to be the first golf course in Jamaica; (length 2000 yards: par 35). Guests are allowed to use the facilities.

Mrs Stephenson's Garden
25 New Green Road, Mandeville.   Tel: 809-962-2328.
Tours of this beautiful garden with orchids, anthurium, ortaniques, etc., can be arranged with Mrs Carmen Stephenson, herself acting as guide. She is a proud winner of many prizes from the annual Manchester Horticultural Show held in Mandeville at the end of May. Donation: J$10.00 per person.

St Marks, Mandeville Parish Church
Of special note is St Marks Anglican (Mandeville Parish Church) – about 1817. From the air, one is able to see that the church was built in the shape of a cross. During the many revolts before emancipation it was sometimes used as a jail. The church is surrounded by many tombs. The oldest dated grave is 1856.

SWA Craft Centre

The Centre provides short-term occupation for girls who have some skills but are unemployed. Products include fine embroidery and crochet work, toys such as the Jamaican equivalent of the Cabbage Patch Doll; also clothing, pastry, cakes and sweets.

Centre opens Monday to Friday, 9:00 a.m. to 4:00 p.m.

Visit a Great House

Marshall's Pen Great House

In 1795 the Marshall's Pen property, together with Shooter's Hill and Martin's Hill, were bought by the Earl of Balcarres, Governor of the Island, as a going concern. There appears to have been a large acreage in coffee. The dry work was done in the lower part of the house, bringing the product to the stage when the unroasted beans were bagged, ready for shipment from Alligator Pond. The huge wooden wheel which rubbed the parchment skin off the beans is still there, but no longer in the house.

After 1939 when the Marshall's Pen property was purchased by the father of A.W. Sutton, communication between the upper and lower floors by means of a staircase, which was then built, was established. The high ceilings show that the original roof covering was hand-hewn shingles. An attempt has been made to furnish the house with pieces of furniture as close as possible to the furniture of the period when it was built.

The house contains portraits of members of the Sutton family. They include Robert Sutton, one of the founders of the London Stock Exchange, and a member of the Mercers' Company of London, his oldest son, also Robert Sutton and his wife, Harriet *née* Ludlow, their son, Robert Sutton, and the grandfather of A.W. Sutton who was Archdeacon of Lewes in Sussex, England. There is also a photograph of Leonard Sutton, Mr A. Sutton's father. The latter was the first member of the family to come to Jamaica, although the family had owned estates here since 1844. Other portraits are those of Mr A. Sutton's grandmother and of her father, Bishop Gilbert, Michael Muirhead and his wife. Mr Muirhead's grandson, another Michael Muirhead, bought the property around 1853 and the family lived there for approximately three generations.

For a tour of the property: Tel: 809-962-2260.
Donation: J$30.00 per person.

Bird watching at Marshall's Pen

Marshall's Pen is a cattle property and nature reserve, situated about three miles from the town of Mandeville. In the well-established woodlands and pastures, 89 of Jamaica's 256 species of birds may be observed. These include 23 of the island's 27 endemic species. A total of 51 species of birds breed on the property. Many of Jamaica's endemic reptiles, amphibians, insects, ferns and trees can also be seen here.

Bird watchers are invited to visit Marshall's Pen by appointment only. The best times to see birds are between 6:00 a.m. and 9:00 a.m., and between 4:00 p.m. and 6:00 p.m. There are many property roads and paths which may be used for self-guided tours.

If you are planning to visit Marshall's Pen, please contact Ann or Robert Sutton in advance, Tel: 809-962-2260.

A small charge is made to help cover costs. Special tours, guided by an experienced naturalist, can be arranged for groups.
If you visit Marshall's Pen, **please**
- close all gates;
- do not climb on stone walls;
- do not light fires;
- do not collect plants;
- take your litter away.

Exploring inland Jamaica

The tours suggested here take us through inland Jamaica and through the island's past. We see the physical features as well as diverse aspects of the way of life. We pass through typical limestone country which, for long ages, was submerged beneath the sea. We pass within hailing distance of peasants tilling the land beneath the gaudy sun, planting Irish potatoes. The first tour takes us through country that was developed in the early period of Jamaica's history. The second gives us an insight into the achievement of the Jamaican people.

Mandeville – Milk river – Old plantations

Leave Mandeville by the A2 and travel by way of Williamsfield, down Melrose Hill, through Porus to Toll Gate. At Toll Gate turn right, on to B12, and continue by way of St Jago and then to Milk River Spa.

Milk River Spa

Some time ago, at the invitation of the Government of Jamaica, a team of consultants from West Germany visited the island and analysed the waters of fifteen mineral springs. Their report shows that the island has, in most of these springs, a very valuable and hitherto neglected resource. The three major spas are those at Milk River, at Bath in the parish of St Thomas, and at Sans Souci on the north coast near Ocho Rios. These three spas are being developed.

The report confirmed earlier analyses of the water of the Milk River Spa, that, therapeutically, it was more efficacious than the waters of Baden or Vichy and that its radio-activity was many times greater than theirs. Many Jamaicans suffering from rheumatic complaints and arthritis have found the waters of the Spa highly beneficial.

The Milk River is a slow-moving stream that flows through flat land, part of Jamaica's largest plain which stretches from Kingston west into the parish of Clarendon, and to the Manchester hills. Clarendon, one of the island's largest parishes, has an area of 487 square miles. In the north, around Frankfield and Chapelton, are the mountains. The most conspicuous is the Bull Head Mountain, 3600 feet high, standing at the centre of Jamaica. The chief physical feature is the Round Hill in Vere.

The plain has some tobacco and sisal, cattle and sugar-cane, and one of Jamaica's largest sugar factories, Monymusk. The north has citrus and a variety of foodcrops.

The large expanse of flat land, the fertile soil and excellent climate of the north attracted settlers from the very beginning of English colonisation in 1655.

The healing waters of the Spa will attract more and more visitors as they become widely known. Visitors will enjoy exploring upper Clarendon for the beauty of its landscape, its excellent climate and its historic associations.

Old plantations tour

This tour can be made from the Milk River Spa, and also from Kingston or Mandeville. Start from the Spa, and proceed by way of Milk River and the B12 through Springfield, Race Course, Alley, Lionel Town, Dawkins Pen and Salt River to join the A2 at Freetown, and then continue to Old Harbour. Alley Church, built in 1715, has some old monuments. The Salt River is used for transporting sugar. Port Esquivel, near Old Harbour, is a bauxite port built for shipping Alcan's alumina.

From Old Harbour onwards let Leonard Sutton be your guide. One of his ancestors was among the first English settlers. His descendants run the gracious property Marshall's Pen, near Mandeville, with three hundred acres of cattle country, hiking trails, horseback riding, a bird sanctuary, a wild garden and a charming Great House with valuable antique furniture. Marshalls Pen has limited accommodation for guests. Those who love nature and history will find it a refreshing, hospitable place.

After leaving Old Harbour this route leads through the part of the country which was settled shortly after the conquest of the island in 1655 by Englishmen of historic fame such as Colbeck, Morant, Pennant, Collier, Long, Wildman, Sutton, Dawkins, Beckford, Bright, Penrhyn, Gale, Sinclair, Morgan, and in many instances their names are still preserved in the names of the properties they owned.

The first point of interest is the ruin of Colbeck Castle. This is the only moat-surrounded fortress in the island, and was erected by Colonel Colbeck who came to Jamaica with Penn and Venables at the time of the conquest (1655) . . . Next on the route comes Sevens Plantation, settled by Anthony Collier who was a member of the first Council (1671), then Longville, settled by Samuel Long who also came with Penn and Venables in 1655. He found on the banks of the Rio Minho, which flows through the property, basins where the Indians and later the Spaniards washed for gold. A mile or so further on and skirting the river the old sugar works of Moore's Hall are to be seen . . .

Retreat is the next point of interest. It belonged to the wealthy Beckford Family, one of whom was Lord Mayor of

London. This was also a sugar plantation. Some copper mining has been done on the property.

Leaving Retreat, the Bull Head, the highest point in this particular mountain range, soon comes into view . . . it marks the centre of the island. Kellets, famed for its beautiful cut stone ruins, which lie beneath, was settled by Moses Kellet . . .

On approaching Rock River village the fine aqueduct and works of the sugar estate Rock River, with its charming surroundings of hills, valley, river and tobacco fields, present an extraordinarily beautiful view. A mile further on the Rio Minho is crossed . . . and the road leads on past the sugar works of Low Ground which at one time was owned by the Wildman family of Chilham Castle, Kent. A lovely view of the Minho valley is obtained from the road above the works, also of Suttons Plantation, formerly owned by Colonel Thomas Sutton who commanded the Militia and repulsed the French Admiral Du Casse in 1694 at Carlisle Bay. The property eventually came into the possession of his kinsman Henry Dawkins whose crest is carved on the doorway of the old boiling house. The motto is 'Strike, Dawkins, strike, the Devil's in the hemp.'

Leaving Chapelton, the route passes through the sugar plantations of Danks and Savoy, formerly in the possession of the Beckford Family. It is worthy of note that Colonel Beckford, who lived at Danks, was appointed to allot land to form the city of Kingston after the great earthquake of 1692. Beckford Street, Kingston, was named after him in 1702. Morgans Valley, close by, was in the possession of the famous buccaneer Morgan, who later in life was knighted and became Governor of Jamaica in 1678.

Mandeville to Ocho Rios by way of Williamsfield – Walderston – Spaldings – Borobridge – Cave Valley – Alexandria – Brown's Town – Discovery Bay – St Anns Bay – Ocho Rios

General

The tour takes us across central Jamaica to the north coast. It passes through a countryside of great natural beauty, and in the course of it the story of Jamaica unfolds before our eyes.

From Mandeville to Brown's Town we pass through typical limestone country. There are few rivers. The streams disappear underground, pass through a maze of caverns and reappear at the edge of the escarpment, nearer to the sea.

The land alternates between rolling pastures with rounded hills and hollows and steep jagged outcrops of razor-edged limestone. The soil is generally poor and difficult to cultivate because of the lack of water. Fields of yam, sweet potatoes and plantains appear where there are pockets of soil, but pasture-lands prevail. Pictured in the landscape is the two-tier system of Jamaican agriculture, with small holdings of under five acres and large properties of one hundred acres or more. A major problem becomes clear – that the number of small farms is growing, while the number of medium-sized farmers is declining and the large farmers remain much the same. 'More people', says a recent review, 'have to be supported by less land in cultivation'.

The large holdings include estates, plantations and pens. The sugar estates, combinations of field and factory, acquired the fertile plains and penetrated inland along river valleys where the land was good and most of it low-lying. Then came plantations of coffee, pimento and, later, bananas. Estates and plantations produced primarily for export. Alongside them, but on less fertile land and generally in more remote areas, came the pens which produced for the local market.

As we drive from Walderston and Spaldings through Cave Valley and Alexandria to Brown's Town and on to Discovery Bay, we see the three types of large holdings. The three were all tied together in a complex inter-related system of agricultural production, the estates and plantations producing for overseas markets and the pens aiming at the local market. Working cattle, horses, asses and mules were all raised for sale to estates and plantations where they were used to power mills and to transplant goods and people. The pens also purchased worn-out working cattle from estates and plantations and fattened them for the local market.

Three key points on our route are:

Spaldings, fifteen miles north of Mandeville, which has in Knox College an innovative, outward-reaching educational complex ranging from an infant school to a Community College. In the 1940s an innovative Scotsman, a Presbyterian parson, Lewis Davidson and his wife Jean, set about transforming two rugged limestone hills into an educational centre planned to meet the needs of rural Jamaica. Knox College gradually took shape, and today ranks as one of Jamaica's most enterprising educational ventures.

Cave Valley lies twenty miles beyond Spaldings, near an old Maroon base on the 'Red Lands' savannah, called by early Spanish colonists 'Los Bermejales', later corrupted into 'Vera Ma Hollis'.

Nearby are the Cave River Sinks, into which the Cave River disappears. It makes its way through underground caverns and rises again thirteen miles farther north, at Riverhead near Stewart Town. The records show that in exceptionally rainy seasons the Cave River and Yankee Rivers, usually almost insignificant streams, have reached levels of over seventy-five feet. The heavy rainfalls of June 1966, for example, led to the flooding of the Cave Valley village to a depth of twelve feet.

Brown's Town is a charming country town with a personality of its own. It lies near the point where our route begins its descent down the escarpment to the coast at Discovery Bay. The economy, long based on cattle-rearing and the cultivation of ground provisions, was greatly strengthened by the activities in both mining and farming of the Kaiser Bauxite Company, whose office is at Discovery Bay.

The odds are that, as the visitor approaches Brown's Town, he will notice groups of school children, neat in their school uniforms, on their way to basic schools, and to primary and secondary schools in the town. Like Spaldings and a number of other country towns, Brown's Town, with its schools and community college, provides encouraging evidence of the expansion of educational opportunity throughout the island. Jamaica has now achieved universal primary education. It has also diversified its secondary level schools and is both diversifying and expanding its tertiary level institutions.

As we near the north coast it is well to bear in mind that we have traversed what was largely an empty wilderness a century-and-a-half ago. We have driven through Jamaica's heartland, where many of the names of villages and of churches remind us of the struggle to abolish slavery and of the settlement of free villages.

| Appendix |
A visitor's ABC

Access to information

Advance planning takes the hassle out of travel. Good planning makes a vacation a worthwhile investment.

The first step is to find a source of up-to-date information. Contact a reliable travel agent or get in touch with the Jamaica Tourist Board, a government agency set up to promote tourism in Jamaica and to help visitors with advice and information.

The Board will send to you free of cost lists of hotels, guest houses, resort catalogues and attractive brochures about the island, its resort centres, cultural and sporting activities, entertainment and investment.

The Board's head office overseas is at 866 Second Avenue, 10th Floor, New York, N.Y. 10017. There are other offices in the USA, Canada, the United Kingdom and Western Europe.

Visitors should get as much information as possible about the hotel or apartment, its location, whether it is on or near the beach; how far it is from a shopping centre and the airport; whether there are arrangements with other hotels for dining or interchange of meals; how near it is to a bank or to medical facilities; what credit cards are accepted. It is a serious offence under Jamaican law to make any purchases except in Jamaican dollars (J$); this includes taxi fares. The exception is goods purchased In Bond.

Airlines

Among the airlines serving Jamaica are the national airline, Air Jamaica, Aeroflot, Air Canada, American Airlines, ALM, British Airways, BWIA, Cayman Airways, Continental, COPA, Cubana, Eastern and Northwest. There are also numerous charters from North America and Europe.

Millionaire's Row, Port Antonio [JAMAICA TOURIST BOARD]

Banks

Banking facilities are available in all towns. Banking hours are from 9:00 a.m. to 2:30 p.m. from Monday to Thursday and on Fridays from 9:00 a.m. to 3:00 p.m. Banks are closed on Saturdays and Sundays and all public holidays.

Cars, driving licence

Self-drive cars, limousines, buses and taxis are available. Self-drive cars can be hired from a number of car-rental companies. The best way to free yourself from dependence on others is to hire a car, not by any means expensive for visitors from overseas, the exchange rates being in their favour.

Jamaica has more than 6000 miles of road. All major roads are asphalted. Dirt roads should be approached with caution. There are garage and service facilities in every township. If you decide to rent a car you might wish to consider taking out temporary memberhip with the Jamaica Automobile Association.

Efficient limousine and bus services link the major resort areas.

The hotel desk can furnish details.

Some taxis and private-hire cars are not metered. Always check rates, whether metered or not. If you plan making a return journey by the same vehicle make sure that the amount quoted covers the return journey. Drivers are reliable and courteous. Many have had long experience in looking after visitors and serve as very efficient guides.

Bear in mind that cars drive on the left and overtake on the right.

Also, in tropical countries such as Jamaica roads are used for much more than travelling from one place to another. The road reflects the way of life, and may serve as a meeting place, or a cricket pitch for small boys. In consequence, motorists use the horn more frequently than in northern countries, to warn pedestrians of their approach.

Driving licences: citizens of Canada, the USA and the United Kingdom should bring their driving licences with them for they are recognised as valid in the island. Show it to the staff member of the company from whom you hire the car. He will tell you what formalities if any, should be observed.

Entry requirements, passports, visas

If you are coming from a country where there is yellow fever, you will be asked to present a valid yellow fever vaccination certificate. You must have had the vaccination at least ten days before arriving in Jamaica but less than ten years. This is because the yellow fever certificate is valid for only ten years.

Passports are not required from citizens and legal residents of the United States or Canada but they must have proof of citizenship or legal residence, such as a passport (not expired beyond one year), birth certificate (married women also need marriage certificate), voter registration card or naturalisation papers. Except for passport, at least two of the above documents must be produced, one of which should be a photographic ID. Visas are not required by citizens of Commonwealth countries for a stay of up to six months but they must have valid passports. Citizens of certain European countries may also enter as tourists with valid passports but no visas for stays

Rafting on the Rio Grande *opposite* [JAMAICA TOURIST BOARD, NEW YORK]

of up to 90 days, among them citizens of West Germany, Austria, Belgium, Switzerland, Sweden, Turkey, Norway, Denmark, Finland, Italy and San Marino, Iceland, Liechtenstein, Luxembourg, and the Netherlands. This also applies to Mexicans. Citizens of Japan need valid passports but no visas for a stay of up to 30 days. In all cases, visitors must have return or onward tickets and the proper documentation required for entry into the country to which they are going after leaving Jamaica.

Public holidays

These are New Year's Day, Ash Wednesday, Good Friday, Easter Monday, National Labour Day (May 23), Independence Day (First Monday in August), National Heroes' Day (3rd Monday in October), Christmas Day, Boxing Day (December 26).

Health and medication

Jamaica is a healthy country. It has an excellent public health service. It is free from many of the diseases that afflict tropical countries. In the 1940s tuberculosis was eradicated. An island-wide system of water purification, including filtering, chlorination and the provision of piped water, has eliminated typhoid. Malaria is controlled by a spraying programme.

There is a programme for children under two, involving immunisation against measles. International organisations and the development agencies of a number of countries have been supplementing the efforts of the Government and the Jamaican Community to keep public health at its present high level.

Shopping: in bond, free port, good buys

In Jamaica, only Jamaican currency is legal tender except for 'in bond' or, 'duty free' purchases which must be paid for in foreign currency. You may take delivery of all 'in bond' or 'duty free' purchases (except liquor and cigarettes) or you may direct that these be sent to the delivery counter at the airport.

If you are a **United States citizen** you can take US$300 worth of goods (based on fair retail value) after staying for 48 hours outside the United States. Members of a family, including infants, may combine exemptions. Declarations may be made by one member. Above this amount duty may be charged.

If you are over 21 years of age, you may take with you one litre of alcoholic beverage. Above this quantity, duty will be charged.

You are allowed to mail to the United States **gifts** valued up to US$25 (fair retail value) free of US duty, but these gifts **must not** include liquor, perfume, cigars and cigarettes. The gifts will not affect the US$300 exemption.

Freeport stores will attend to the mailing. You are allowed to mail an unlimited number of such duty free gifts, provided that the addressee does not receive more than US$25 worth in one day. You cannot send a duty free parcel to yourself.

If you are a **Canadian citizen**, you are allowed to take in to Canada C$25 worth of goods free of Canadian duty, after you have stayed 48 hours outside Canada. The accumulated value of such goods cannot exceed C$75 per calendar quarter. Excess (but only up to C$150) is subject to 25 per cent duty. After seven days absence, goods valued at C$300 can be brought in duty free once in each calendar year.

MACMILLAN CARIBBEAN GUIDES SERIES
Other titles available

Dyde: *Antigua and Barbuda: The Heart of the Caribbean*
Saunders: *The Bahamas: A Family of Islands*
Hoyos: *Barbados: The Visitor's Guide*
Raine: *The Islands of Bermuda: Another World*
Gravette: *Cuba: Official Guide*
Halabi: *Curaçao Close-Up*
Honychurch: *Dominica: Isle of Adventure*
Sinclair: *Grenada: Isle of Spice*
Dyde: *Islands to the Windward: Five Gems of the Caribbean (St Maarten/St Martin, St Barts, St Eustatius, Saba, Anguilla)*
Sherlock and Preston: *Jamaica: The Fairest Isle, A Visitor's Guide*
Fergus: *Monserrat: Emerald Isle of the Caribbean*
Gordon: *Nevis: Queen of the Caribees*
Dyde: *St Kitts: Cradle of the Caribbean*
Ellis: *St Lucia: Helen of the West Indies*
Taylor: *Trinidad and Tobago: A Guide and Introduction*
Smithers: *The Turks and Caicos Islands: Lands of Discovery*
Shepard: *The British Virgin Islands: Treasure Islands of the Caribbean*